Finding Alphas

FINDING ALPHAS

A Quantitative Approach to Building Trading Strategies

Igor Tulchinsky et al.
WorldQuant Virtual Research Center

WILEY

Dedicated to All at WorldQuant —

The Future of Trading

Contents

Preface

This book is a study of the process of finding alphas. The material is presented as a collection of essays, providing diverse viewpoints from successful quants on the front lines of quantitative trading.

A wide variety of topics is covered, ranging from theories about the existence of alphas, to the more concrete and technical aspects of alpha creation.

Part I presents a general introduction to alpha creation, and is followed by a brief account of the alpha life-cycle, and insights on cutting losses.

Part II focuses more on the technical side of alpha design, such as the dos and don'ts of information research, key steps to developing an alpha, and the evaluation and improvement of quality alphas. The key technical aspects discussed in this section are turnover, backtesting, fundamental analysis, equity price volume, statistical arbitrage, overfitting, and alpha diversity.

Part III explores *ad hoc* topics in alpha design, including alpha design for various asset classes like futures and currencies, the development of momentum alphas, and the effect of news and social media on stock returns.

In Part IV, we introduce you to WebSim™, a web-based alpha development tool. We invite all quant enthusiasts to utilize this free tool to learn about alpha backtesting (also known as alpha simulation), and ultimately to create their own alphas.

Finally, in Part V, we present an inspirational essay for all quants who are ready to explore the world of quantitative trading.

Acknowledgments

In these pages, we present readers with a collection of writings on the alchemic art of finding alphas. It is written by WorldQuant's founder, directors, managers, in-house portfolio managers, and quantitative researchers. The key objectives of this collection are twofold – to present many viewpoints as to how to define an alpha, and how to find one. At WorldQuant, we believe no viewpoint is the best and only answer, and that a variety of approaches is always superior to a single one. We also present our online financial markets simulation tool known as WebSim™, which lets users and consultants create, test, simulate, and track alphas.

WorldQuant would like to thank Rohit Agarwal, Ionut Aron, Pankaj Bakliwal, Scott Bender, Hongzhi Chen, Benjamin Ee, Zhuangxi Fang, Paul A. Griffin, Yongfeng He, Richard Hu, Yu Huang, Hammad Khan, Michael Kozlov, Geoffrey Lauprete, Cong Li, Weijia Li, Zhiyu Ma, Sunny Mahajan, Pratik Patel, Kailin Qi, Jeffrey Scott, Xinye Tang, Swastik Tiwari, Igor Tulchinsky, Peng Wan, Richard Williams, Peng Yan, and Wancheng Zhang for their contributions, polishing efforts, and time invested in making this book a reality.

A special note of thanks to Wendy Goldman Rohm, our literary agent, for her critical and insightful comments on early drafts, her awesome proofing, and many great suggestions throughout the project; and to Werner Coetzee and the teams at John Wiley and Sons for their expert guidance and detailed and helpful advice. Many thanks also to Jeffrey Blomberg and Kristin Chach, WorldQuant's most dedicated legal team, for their wise counsel and tireless work to keep us on the track and guide us beyond. And thanks to Tracy Tseung for her timely project management and editorial assistance.

Finally, we would like to acknowledge with gratitude the support and faith of every colleague at WorldQuant. Thank you all.

DISCLAIMER

The contents of this book are intended for informational and educational purposes only and, as such, are not intended to be nor should be construed in any manner to be investment advice. The views expressed are those of the various contributors and do not necessarily reflect the view or opinion of WorldQuant or WorldQuant Virtual Research Center.

About the WebSim™ Website

At the time of writing, the WebSim™ information contained in this document is consistent with the WebSim™ website. Since the website is subject to change, in cases where there exist inconsistencies between this document and the website, the terms of the WebSim™ website will govern the most updated and current processes of WebSim™. For the most up-to-date version of WebSim™ and the terms applicable to use of WebSim™, please go to https://websim.worldquantchallenge.com or its successor site.

Registration at WebSim's™ official website is required to obtain the full functionality of the tool, and to have access to the WebSim™ support team. Successful alphas may, in certain cases, be considered for inclusion in actual quant trading investment strategies managed by WorldQuant.

WEBSIM™ RESEARCH CONSULTANTS

WorldQuant has established a Research Consultant program for qualified individuals to work with our web-based simulation platform, WebSim. This program gives consultants the flexibility to create alphas in their own physical and intellectual environment. This is a particularly ideal pursuit for individuals who are undertaking college education as well as those who are ambitious and highly interested in breaking into the financial industry.

Qualified candidates are those highly quantitative individuals who typically come from STEM (Science, Technology, Engineering, or Mathematics) programs. Actual majors and expertise vary and may include Statistics, Financial Engineering, Mathematics, Computer Science, Finance, Physics, or other various STEM programs.

You can find more details on WebSim™ in Part IV of this book. Full Research Consultant program information is also available at WebSim's™ official website.

PART I
Introduction

1
Introduction to Alpha Design
By Igor Tulchinsky

An alpha is a combination of mathematical expressions, computer source code, and configuration parameters that can be used, in combination with historical data, to make predictions about future movements of various financial instruments. An alpha is also a forecast of the return on each of the financial securities. An alpha is also a fundamentally based opinion. The three definitions are really equivalent. Alphas definitely exist, and we design and trade them. This is because even if markets are near-efficient, *something* has to make them so. Traders execute alpha signals, whether algorithmic, or fundamental. Such activity moves prices, pushing them towards efficiency point.

HOW ARE ALPHAS REPRESENTED?

An alpha can be represented as a matrix of securities and positions indexed by time. The value of the matrix corresponds to positions in that particular stock on that particular day. Positions in stock change daily; the daily changes are traded in the securities market. The alpha produces returns, and returns have variability. The ratio of return to standard deviation (variability) of the returns is the information ratio of the alpha. It so happens that the information ratio of the alpha is maximized when alpha stock positions are proportional to the forecasted return of that stock.

Expressions and Programs

Alphas can be represented by expressions consisting of variables or programs. Such expressions, or programs, are equivalent to each other, meaning one can always be converted to the other.

HOW DOES ONE DESIGN AN ALPHA BASED ON DATA?

It is simple. A price action is a response to some world event. This event is reflected in the data. If the data never changes then there is no alpha. Thus, it is changes in the data that have the information. A change in information should produce a change in the alpha.

Changes may be characterized in many ways as can be seen in Table 1.1.

Table 1.1   Expression of changes

A simple difference, A – B	Example: today's_price – yesterday's_price
A ratio, A/B	Example: today's_price/yesterday's_price
An expression	Example: 1/today's price. Increase position when price is low

All alpha design is the intelligent search of the space for all possible changes. An expression should express a hypothesis. Examples of this can be seen in Table 1.2.

Table 1.2   Expressions expressed as a hypothesis

Expression	Hypothesis
1/price	Invest more if price is low
Price-delay (price,3)	Price moves in the direction of 3-day change
Price	High-priced stocks go higher
Correlation (price,delay(price,1))	Stocks that trend, outperform
(price/delay(price,3)) * rank(volume)	Trending stocks with increasing volume outperform

QUALITY OF AN ALPHA

An alpha is considered one of good quality when:

- The idea and expression is simple.
- The expression/code is elegant.
- It has good in-sample Sharpe.
- It is not sensitive to small changes in data and parameters.

- It works in multiple universes.
- It works in different regions.
- Its profit hits a recent new high.

ALGORITHM FOR FINDING ALPHAS

Repeat the below steps forever:

- Look at the variables in the data.
- Get an idea of the change you want to model.
- Come up with a mathematical expression that translates this change into stock position.
- Test the expression.
- If the result is favorable, submit the alpha.

2
Alpha Genesis – The Life-Cycle of a Quantitative Model of Financial Price Prediction

By Geoffrey Lauprete

An alpha is a model that predicts the prices of financial instruments. And while the idea of modeling the markets and predicting prices was not new back in the 1980s and 1990s, it was during that era that cheap computing power became a reality, making possible both (1) computational modeling on Wall Street trading desks, and (2) the generation and collection of data at a rate that is still growing exponentially as of the writing of this chapter. As computers and systematic data collection became ubiquitous, the need for innovative modeling techniques that could use these newly-created data became one of the drivers of the migration of PhDs to Wall Street. Finally, it was in this climate of technology evolution and exponential data production that the quantitative trading industry was born.

BACKGROUND

Quantitative trading and alpha research took off at the same time that cheap computational power became available on Wall Street. Alphas are predictions that are used as inputs in quantitative trading. Another way of putting it is to say that quantitative trading is the monetization of the alphas. Note that an alpha, as a form of prediction model, is not the same thing as a pure arbitrage. Sometimes the term statistical arbitrage is used to describe quantitative trading that exploits alphas.

Note that one could debate whether alphas ought to exist at all – some of the arguments for and against the existence of alphas can be made as part of an "efficient market hypothesis." The financial economics academic literature tackles this problem exhaustively, qualifying the markets and the nature of information flow, and deriving conclusions based on various assumptions on the markets, the market participants and their level of rationality, and how the participants interact and process information.

That said, from a simple intuitive perspective, it makes sense that a very complex system such as the markets would exhibit some level of predictability. Whether these predictions can form the basis of exploitable opportunities is the argument that the quantitative trading industry is making every day, with more or less success.

CHALLENGES

Even if one can make an argument in favor of the existence of alphas under various stylized assumptions, the details of prediction in the real world are messy. A prediction with low accuracy, or a prediction that estimates a weak price change, may not be interesting from a practitioner's perspective. The markets are an aggregate of people's intentions, affected by changing technology, macro-economic reality, regulations, and wealth – which makes the business of prediction more challenging than meets the eye. Thus, to model the markets, one needs a strong understanding of the exogenous variables that affect the prices of financial instruments.

THE LIFE-CYCLE OF ALPHAS

A fundamental law of the markets is that any potentially profitable strategy attracts attention and attracts capital. Since the markets are a finite size, when more capital chases a strategy or employs a particular alpha, this implies that the fixed-sized pie that constituted the original opportunity needs to be sliced into multiple thinner slices. The end result is that, while alphas are born from the interaction of market participants, when they are (1) strong enough, (2) old enough, and (3) consistent enough to be statistically validated and provide the basis for profitable trading strategies, they will begin to attract capital. This capital flow will ensure that the alpha will shrink and become more volatile, until there is so much capital chasing the idea that it will stop working. However, this process will affect the markets in ways that create other patterns, perpetuating the cycle of birth and death of alphas.

DATA INPUT

In order to predict the price movement of financial instruments, alphas need data. This data can be the prices themselves or a historical record of those prices. Most of the time, however, it helps to have more information than just the prices. For example, how many shares of a stock were traded, its volume, etc., can complement the historical price–time series.

A simple diagram to represent what an alpha is doing is as follows:

DATA (E.G. HISTORICAL PRICES) → ALPHA → PRICE PREDICTION

Note that data quality can have a large effect on the output of an alpha. So it's important to evaluate data quality before it is used and address shortcomings then. Issues that may affect data quality can be technical, e.g. hardware problems, or related to human error, e.g. unexpected data format change, extra digits, etc.

PREDICTIVE OUTPUT

An alpha model's output is typically a prediction. In many markets, it's easier to predict the relative price of a financial instrument than it is to predict the absolute price of a financial instrument. Thus, in stocks, many alpha models predict the movement of the prices of various stocks relative to other similar stocks.

Typically, alphas are implemented using a programming language like C++, Python, or any other flexible and modern language. In larger organizations, a software environment developed in-house can abstract the alpha developer from many book-keeping and data management issues, letting the developer focus on creative research and modeling.

EVALUATION

What is a good alpha? What is a bad one? There is no single metric that will answer that question. In addition, the answer depends in part on how the alpha is going to be used. Certain investment strategies require very strong predictors; others benefit, marginally, from weak ones. Some pointers to alpha evaluation are:

- Good in-sample performance doesn't guarantee good out-of-sample performance.
- Just like in academic statistics, outliers can ruin a model and lead to erroneous predictions.

It takes a lot of in-sample and out-of-sample testing to validate an idea. The more data one has, the more confidence one can have in an alpha. Conversely, the longer the period one considers, the more likely that the alpha will exhibit signs of decay and the more likely fundamental market changes will make the alpha unusable in the future. Thus, there is a natural tension between developing confidence in an alpha and its usefulness. One must strike the right balance.

LOOKING BACK

When developing alphas, one has the opportunity to look back in time and evaluate how certain predictive models would have performed historically. And, while evaluating an alpha with backtesting is invaluable (providing a window into both the markets and how the alpha would have performed), there are a few important points to remember:

- History never repeats itself exactly, ever. So while an alpha idea may look great on paper, there's no guarantee it will continue to work in the future. This is because of the perverse power of computation, and the ability of creative modelers to miss the forest for the trees. With computational resources, one can evaluate a very large number of ideas and permutations of those ideas. But without the discipline to keep track of what ideas were tried, and without taking that into account when evaluating the likelihood of a model being a true model versus a statistical artifact only, one will end up mistaking lumps of coal for gold.

- It's easy to look back at history and imagine that the market was easier to trade than it was in reality. That's because of several effects. First, you didn't have the insight back then that you have now. In addition, you didn't have the data back then that you have now. Finally, you didn't have the computational power and technology to do what you can do now. Ideas that seem simple and were programmed in spreadsheets in the 1990s were actually not so simple back then, especially when one considers the research it took to get there. Every decade has its market and its own unique market opportunities. It's up to the alpha developer to find market opportunities with the data and technology available. Looking back at previous eras, it is wrong to believe it would have been easy to predict the market and make money.

STATISTICS! = STATISTICAL ARBITRAGE

The term statistical arbitrage is another term used to describe quantitative investing. The term conjures a couple of ideas: (1) that the predictions used don't constitute a pure and risk-free arbitrage, and (2) that statistical models are used to predict prices. While (1) is absolutely correct, (2) requires some explanation. While it is the case that certain models from academic statistics – such as time series analysis and machine learning, or regression and optimization – can be used as part of alpha development, it's important to realize that most techniques from academia aren't really aiming to solve the problem that is of interest to a quantitative investment firm (i.e., generating a cash flow and managing the risk of that cash flow). Thus, while looking at mean-square errors when evaluating models has some merit, it is only indirectly related to making money.

TO SUM IT UP

The existence of alphas in the market is a result of the imperfect flow of information among market participants with competing objectives. An investor with a long-term horizon may not be concerned with short-term variations in price. Conversely, a trader with a short-term horizon doesn't need to understand the fundamental factors affecting price movements, and is rewarded for understanding short-term supply-and-demand dynamics instead. Yet these different investors coexist and arguably provide some value to the other. In addition, each investor's actions in the market coalesce to produce patterns. The goal of an alpha researcher is to find which of these patterns are relevant to predicting future prices, subject to various constraints, like the availability of data and the researcher's modeling toolkit. While the nature of the alphas changes with time, it is the researcher's challenge to find which ideas are relevant today, and to implement them in a way that is efficient, robust, and elegant.

3
Cutting Losses
By Igor Tulchinsky

Man is a creature who became successful because he was able to make sense of his environment and apply rules more effectively than all his other competitors. In hunting and agriculture and, later, physics, the understanding of rules proliferated as man advanced. Today the mastering of rules abounds in every area. From finance to exercise, to relationships and self-improvement, rules describe it all. Man depends on rules.

There are an infinite number of possible rules that describe reality, and the mind of man is always struggling and working to discover more and more. Yet, paradoxically, there is only one rule governing them all. That rule is: no rule ever works perfectly. We call it the "UnRule."

As a matter of fact, it is a scientific principle that no rule can really be proved, it can only be disproved. It was Karl Popper, the great philosopher of science, who pointed this out in 1934. He said it is impossible to verify a universal truth; instead, a single counter-instance could disprove it. Popper stressed that, because pure facts don't exist, all observations and rules are subjective and theory laden.

There is good reason why rules can't be proved. Reality is complicated. People and their ideas are imperfect. Ideas are expressed as abstractions, in words or symbols. Rules are just metaphorical attempts to get at reality. Thus, every rule is flawed and no rule works all the time. No single dogma describes or rules the world. But every rule describes the world a little bit. And every rule works, sometimes.

We are like artists who gradually paint an image on the canvas. Every stroke brings the image closer to reality, but it never becomes reality and never becomes a perfect interpretation of it. Instead, we get closer and closer to it, never quite reaching it. Examples abound. Newton's laws, which for centuries seemed to describe motion perfectly, turned out to be flawed, giving way to relativity. Man's explanation for himself and his place in the universe has been continually evolving – from the belief that earth was the center of everything, to the realization that we are really specks of dust in something beyond our grasp. Likewise, various rules have been asserted in the world of finance, including option models, only to be shown to be wrong and assumption laden in a meltdown.

And so you see the paradox: the only rule that works is the rule that no rule always works. Rules are just little specks of dust, pointing their way towards reality, but never quite reaching it.

This is the very reason why it is of utmost importance to cut losses when riding the changing sea of UnRules. How can this be mastered? What is the correct way to deal with the millions of shifting rules, all of them imperfect and often conflicting, based on different sets of circumstances and assumptions?

Trading is a microcosm of reality, a dynamic environment of immense complexity in which billions of participants act based on billions of rules and beliefs, which, in turn, affect the environment. The challenge in trading is, of course, to derive the rules that describe the markets, and then use them successfully to earn profits without changing those markets in such a way that the rule itself is destroyed.

Rules in trading are called alphas, and alphas are really little algorithms for predicting the future of securities returns. Managing millions of rules, where each rule is really a hypothesis, is a complicated matter and a subject in itself. When dealing with millions of rules in the realm of trading, certain regularities become apparent. This brings us back to cutting losses. The best, most universal way of dealing with this complexity (and the fact that all rules eventually break down) is by mastering the long-known trading principles behind cutting losses.

In the world of trading, the concept of cutting losses has been around for a long time. It originated in what is possibly the oldest type of trading known as trend-following, in which a bet is made that a rising security will keep rising. In such a scenario, trades are typically entered at a new high and exited when accumulated profits drop more than a certain amount from an all-time high.

In today's trading world, strategies or alphas are seldom as simple as that. Instead of following a particular security, trend following is applied to the accumulated P&L of the strategy.

To put it in plain English and in more general terms: cutting losses simply means letting go of rules that no longer work.

Although the efficacy of cutting losses is very easy to see in the microcosm of trading, its principles hold in many areas of life, including business, entrepreneurship, and relationships.

Cutting losses requires discipline and subjugation of one's ego. Typically, any kind of thinking and decision making, including following rules, can be laden with and distracted by emotion. Brain scientists have seen that people with damage to the brain in the emotional center are unable to make simple decisions like deciding what shirt to put on in the morning. In our work using alphas to make trading decisions, the typical state of mind is driven by an emotional state of confidence. When coming up with a particular strategy, the process starts with, "I understand how the world works, I believe in my rule, here is my rule." Since ego and pride are involved with this confidence, it is hard to let go of the rule one has come up with, even in the face of evidence to the contrary.

Perhaps it is for ego reasons that the principles of cutting losses are not followed more widely. The other reason is lack of knowledge of alternative rules that might be implemented. The high cost of changing one's strategy also contributes to resistance to letting go of rules that no longer work.

It is wise to refrain from believing exclusively in any particular theory or any particular rule. Believe them all. And don't believe any of them completely. Sometimes they work, sometimes they don't.

The best indicator of whether a rule is good is how well it is working at the moment. The rest is speculation. If a rule works, we invest in it; if it doesn't, we don't.

We collect all ideas and let time and performance show what works and what doesn't, and when.

A new idea, rule, or alpha is postulated based on history, and through statistical analysis (with sometimes a touch of fundamental wisdom), it goes into our knowledge base.

From this vast universe of ideas we construct the closest thing possible to a depiction of reality. To do what we do, you have to be comfortable with the fact that you will never know everything there is to know.

They say in the land of the blind, the one-eyed man is king.

And when it comes to trading and financial markets, even having one eye is an accomplishment.

HOW DO WE APPLY THE PRINCIPLE OF THE UNRULE AND OF CUTTING LOSSES?

We acknowledge that the number of imperfect ideas is unbounded, and reality is unknown and unknowable. Each imperfect idea does succeed in describing reality a little bit. So the more alphas we have, the better we can describe an aspect of reality, and the closer we can come to having "one eye" with which we can increase profits.

Since no rule is perfect, a combination of ALL rules comes as close to it as one can.

Applying all rules simultaneously is the key to success. For example, to cross the street, one might have the following rules in mind:

1. Look left, look right, then left again, then it is safe to cross.
2. If you hear a loud noise, turn in the direction of the noise.
3. If you see a car headed towards you, run!

You may start out crossing the street believing in and comforted by Rule 1 when you hear a horn honking, triggering Rule 2. Rule 1 should be cut immediately because the safety conclusion has been challenged by the noise. Then Rule 3 is applied.

So we have the following implications:

• It is necessary to come up with as many good rules as possible.
• No single rule can ever be relied upon completely.
• It is necessary to come up with a strategy for using rules simultaneously.

How do you identify when a strategy is not working? If it performs outside its expected historical returns, signaled when:

• drawdown exceeds what's normal;
• its Sharpe falls;
• it otherwise goes out of the historical box, defying the rules that were initially observed.

It is important to pursue different strategies simultaneously, and to shift one's efforts into working strategies. As a simplified example, suppose one has a theory for describing when gold prices rise. The theory works 50% of the time (years). Suppose one has 10 such equally good theories. A combination of the theories will describe reality better than any one of them. And the best way to manage which one of them is most accurate is by observing which ones are working now.

Then comes the application of cutting losses.

When a strategy stops working, determine the belief that motivated the activity. If the belief was obviously false, you are playing dice here. Best to terminate the activity and engage in more productive ones.

For example, let's say you hire someone to renovate your house. They promise to do the job for $50,000, but less than halfway through the job, they've already spent $45,000. At this point, if switching to a new builder can be done cheaply, cut the old one.

Suppose we are engaged in an activity – let's call it X – which starts to lose money.

The activity can be anything, perhaps a trading strategy or a business. The questions to be asked are:

- Am I losing money in activity X?
- What is the loss amount? Call the loss Z.

Before starting activity X, what was the anticipated amount of the maximum loss? If Z exceeds this amount and the exit cost is not so high, cut the loss.

SUMMARY

Examine each potential action prior to embarking on it.

Determine:

- What's the objective?
- What are the normal, expected difficulties?

Plan in advance how to get out of the strategy cheaply.
Pursue multiple strategies simultaneously.
Cut all strategies that are falling outside expectations.

PART II
Design and Evaluation

4
Alpha Design
By Scott Bender/Yongfeng He

An alpha is a method of making predictions about future asset price changes. For example, an alpha might be a computer program that predicts future returns of a particular set of stocks.

Alphas we cover in this chapter are fully systematic and can be expressed by a concrete piece of code. The alpha will typically make predictions at some periodic frequency, for example, once per day. Its predictions will then be represented by a number for each asset it intends to predict.

A simple alpha might be, for each day, assigning a prediction of +1 to all stocks that went down yesterday and −1 to all stocks that went up. This is a valid alpha for us because it systematically generates a specific prediction for a set of assets at a specific frequency.

Alphas are predictive models, but without a way to implement those predictions, there is no way to realize the potential profits that those predictions might generate. Typically, an alpha is utilized as a component of a trading strategy, which converts the alpha's predictions into actual trading decisions. The strategy is largely driven by the combined predictions of its alphas, but it also considers practical issues such as transaction costs and portfolio risk before actually executing a trade.

CATEGORIZATION OF ALPHAS

Alphas may be categorized into three major groups according to the types of instruments traded, such as stocks, exchange-traded funds, currencies, futures, options and bonds, etc. Alphas may trade single or multiple types of instruments. They could be developed for one specific country or multiple countries combined, or even the global market.

According to the time the alphas use the information, and the frequency at which the predictions are generated, we may categorize those alphas into the following groups:

1. Intraday alphas: rebalanced during trading hours of the day. They can also be grouped as follows:
   a. Rebalance at each interval, e.g. 1 min/5 min/15 min, etc.
   b. Rebalance triggered by some events such as ticks/orders/fills or predefined events.
2. Daily alphas: rebalance every day. These types of alphas can be broken into further subgroups by the time the information is used:
   a. Delay N: use data of N days ago.
   b. Delay 0 snapshot: use the data before a certain time snapshot.
   c. MOO/MOC: alphas trade at market open/close auction session.
3. Weekly/monthly alphas, rebalanced every week/month.

DEVELOPMENT OF AN ALPHA

An alpha is developed by using public information. The more efficient the process, the better performance the alpha can achieve. One can find alphas either by sourcing public information or building specific models to process the information. Alphas can be generated by searching signals/patterns from the informational spaces. Typical sources are as follows:

1. Price/volume. We can use technical analysis or prediction/regression models based on the price/volume.
2. Fundamentals. By analyzing the fundamentals of each company automatically, one can build fundamental alphas. Such alphas typically have very low turnover.
3. Macro data, such as gross domestic product numbers, employment rates. Such numbers have big impacts on the financial markets.
4. Text, such as Federal Open Market Committee minutes, company filings, papers, journals, news, or even information in publicly available social media. It's necessary to quantify the text into numbers (eventually number of shares to buy/sell). Text data includes both current and future events.

5. Multimedia such as videos/audios can also be used as information sources. The techniques to process video/audio are pretty mature. For example, one can simply use Text-To-Speech techniques to extract text information from the video/audio and then build models on the text information.

Sometimes alphas are not derived from the models of information directly. This information may be used to improve the performance of alphas or generate alphas. Some examples are listed below:

1. Risk factor models: by controlling risk exposure or eliminating risk exposure to some factors, one can improve the alpha's performance.
2. Relationship models: e.g. instruments typically correlated with each other to some extent. Some may lead or lag with others, thus they generate the opportunities for arbitrage.
3. Microstructure models to improve the execution performance of real trading.

Today, with information growing explosively, extracting signals from an ever-expanding ocean of noise is more and more challenging. The solution space is non-convex, discontinuous, and dynamic; good signals often arise where least expected. How does one extract such signals? By limiting the search space, using methods previously used by treasure hunters, such as searching in the vicinity of previous discoveries, conserving resources to avoid digging too deeply, and using validated cues to improve the probability of a find. At the same time, always allocate some processing power to test wild ideas.

VALUE OF AN ALPHA

The ultimate test of alpha value is how much risk-adjusted profit it adds to the strategy in which it is trading. However, in practice, this is difficult to measure precisely because:

• There is no canonical strategy in which an alpha may be used, and the exact strategy in which the alpha will be used may not be known at the time of alpha design.

- Even given a level of risk aversion and a specific strategy, there can be non-linear effects in the combination that make it difficult to precisely attribute profit back to individual alphas.
- All that being said, we can still:
  - Make useful predictions about whether an alpha will add value in strategies.
  - Give a reasonable estimate for how much an alpha contributed to the strategy's profit.

PRACTICAL ALPHA EVALUATION

Since we may not know the target trading strategy ahead of time, considering an alpha on its own, how do we know if it is good or bad? Alternatively, when we make a change to an alpha, how do we know if it is an improvement? To answer these questions, we need some measurements that can help us predict if it will add value to a typical strategy.

A typical method for collecting measurements about trading strategies is to run a simulation (i.e. backtest) and measure characteristics, such as information ratio. One way we can make analogous measurements for an alpha is to do a mapping of its predictions to a trading strategy. We can then assume the predictions made by the alpha are positions that a strategy would take in the specific asset. Equivalently, the trades of the strategy would be the change in the alpha's predictions. One issue with this method is that alphas will often not map to good strategies on their own because they are designed to predict returns, not make profitable trades. We can address this by charging zero or very small trading cost in our simulation.

Once we have constructed a simulation such as the one described above, we can now take some measurements:

- **Information ratio**: The mean of the alpha's returns divided by the standard deviation of the returns. Typically, we report this as a daily quantity:
  - Roughly measures how consistently the alpha makes good predictions.
  - The information ratio combined with the length of the observation period can be used to determine how confident we are to determine that the alpha is not some random noise.

- **Margin**: The amount of profit made by the alpha in the simulation divided by the amount of trading that was done:
  - Roughly measures how sensitive the alpha is to transaction costs. Higher margin means that the alpha is not much affected by trading costs.
  - Alphas with low margin will certainly not work as strategies. And they won't add value unless they are very different from the other alphas in the strategy.
- **Uniqueness**: Could be defined as the maximum correlation of the alpha to others in the pool of alphas:
  - Lower correlation will tend to mean that the alpha is more valuable.

More complex tests can also be developed. For example, it can be useful to test if the alpha has good information ratio on both liquid stocks (stocks with high trading volume) and illiquid stocks. If the alpha is only predictive on illiquid stocks, it may have limited usefulness in a strategy that intends to trade at very large size.

FUTURE PERFORMANCE

All of the measurements in the preceding section are intended to compare two alphas where we have no additional information other than their actual predictions. However, additional information, such as how the alpha was constructed, can yield useful information in determining whether the alpha will make good predictions going forward. Ultimately, what is important is whether the alpha makes reliable *future* predictions, not historical predictions.

Suppose we have an alpha with high information ratio, but it was built by taking rules with little economic explanation and optimizing the parameters of said rules to the historical data. For example, suppose the alpha had 12 parameters, one for each month ($x1...x12$), and suppose the alpha rule is simply to buy $x1$ dollars of all stocks in January, $x2$ dollars of all stocks in February, etc. If we optimize $x1–x12$ over the past year, we would get pretty good predictions for last year, but there is no reason to think they would work going into next year.

In general, each optimization or improvement made to an alpha after observing historical data will improve the alpha's historical performance by some amount, and its future performance by some different, usually smaller, amount. Special care should be taken by the alpha designer to ensure that changes are expected to improve the alpha going forward.

When changes to the alpha yield very small (or even negative) improvements to the future predictions compared to large improvements of historical predictions, the alpha is being "overfit" to the historical data. Alpha designers can measure the effect of this overfitting by looking at the performance of their alphas on data that was not used in alpha construction (out-of-sample data) and comparing it to the data used while improving the alpha (in-sample data). Comparison of in-sample to out-of-sample performance is useful not only on the alpha level but also in aggregate across all alphas of a given designer, or on groups of alphas from a given designer. These comparisons on groups of alphas can measure the tendency of a designer's methodology to overfit.

5
How to Develop an Alpha. I: Logic with an Example

By Pankaj Bakliwal

Alphas are mathematical models to predict the future price movements of various financial instruments.

Alpha Logic →Information in the Form of Data → Idea → Mathematical Expression → Apply Operations → Final Robust Alpha → Translate into Positions in Financial Instrument → Check Historical PnL, Other Performance Measurements (Information Ratio, Turnover, Drawdowns, etc.)

The goal is to make profits while minimizing risk, and to develop a mathematical predictive formula by using appropriate information. In order to convert this mathematical formula into stock positions, this formula should have three types of values:

Positive → long position
Negative → Short position
0 → No position

Also, the magnitude of the value derived for each stock from the mathematical formula should be proportional to the dollar amount of the position.

Let's use an example.

STEP 1 → COLLECT INFORMATION

Consider two stocks from the technology sector: Google and Apple. The information is available in the form of daily historical prices of these two stocks. Let's say that we also have information about an upcoming event that would affect the technology companies either in a positive or a negative manner. The second statement has no directional information.

STEP 2 → COME UP WITH AN IDEA

Once we have all the information available, the next step is to come up with a sensible idea. Let's say that based on the historical prices, the observation is that the two stocks have trended upwards during the last week. Logic says that in the absence of any additional information, when stock prices rise, profit booking would take place as investors close their long positions, which in turn pushes the stock prices downward. At the same time, when stock prices fall, investors see an opportunity to buy stocks at a cheaper rate, which in turn pushes the stock prices upwards.

STEP 3 → TRANSLATE INTO A MATHEMATICAL EXPRESSION

Converting a thought into a mathematical formula is not always straightforward. In the above case, though, it can be done as follows:

$$\text{Alpha} = -(1 \text{ week returns}) \tag{1}$$

The negative sign indicates that a short position is taken when the trend is upward, and a long position when the trend is downward.

The dollar amount of long/short position in a particular financial instrument is determined by the magnitude of the formula. This means that the stronger the price trend, the more chances the price will be reverting back.

Let's say the alpha values derived from Eqn (1) for Google and Apple are +2.5 and +7.5, respectively.

STEP 4 → TRANSFORM THE RAW EXPRESSION BY APPLYING OPERATIONS

The raw alpha expression has been developed. The question is: can we make it more robust, more stable? Note that we have one more piece of information – it says there is an upcoming event that would affect the technology companies either in a positive or a negative manner. Can we use this information to make our alpha more profitable?

If our alpha indicates that we should take a long position in both stocks, and the event turns out to be a bad one for the technology sector, thus leading to both the stocks going down drastically, we would end up taking huge losses.

One way to avoid such losses would be to develop a sector-neutral strategy. Such a strategy would not have much downside risk, irrespective of the type of event that is going to occur. A sector-neutral strategy does not have any position in the sector as a whole; i.e. the sum of the positions of the individual stock in the sector is 0. In our example, this would translate to having equal dollar amounts allocated to both the stocks, but in the opposite direction. That is, one would go long one stock and short the other one.

STEP 5 → FINAL ROBUST ALPHA

The final alpha would be a combination derived from both pieces of information. This would change the old values of +2.5 and +7.5 to −5.0 and +5.0 for Google and Apple, respectively.

STEP 6 → TRANSLATE INTO POSITIONS IN A FINANCIAL INSTRUMENT

In order to get the final positions, we can simply apply the following formula:

Final_alpha_stock = (alpha_stock/sum_of_alphas_of_all_stocks) * booksize

So, if we have $10M, we'll go long $5M on Apple and short $5M on Google.

STEP 7 → CHECK FOR ROBUSTNESS

These are indicators for robustness:

1. High in-sample information ratio (IR)
2. Good out-of-sample IR
3. Works well across the trading universe

4. Less fitting
5. Intuitive/interesting/simple idea
6. Works in multiple regions
7. Small drawdowns
8. Short drawdown periods

6
How to Develop an Alpha. II: A Case Study

By Hongzhi Chen

An alpha has multiple definitions. The most widely used definition we use is: a computer algorithm used to predict financial instruments' future movements. Another commonly used term is alpha value, which is the value we assign to each instrument, proportional to the money we use to invest in it. As we talk about alpha, we generally refer to the first definition. When we talk about alpha value, we refer to the second.

Before we talk more about alpha design, let's study a simple example to get a better understanding of what an alpha looks like.

Say we have $1M capital and want to invest continually in a portfolio consisting of two stocks: Google (GOOG) and Apple (AAPL). We need to know how to allocate our capital between these two stocks. If we do a daily rebalance of our portfolio, we need to predict the next few days' return of each stock. How do we do this?

There are a lot of things that can affect the stock prices, such as trader behavior, news, fundamental change, insider behavior, etc. To make things simple, we can deconstruct the prediction process into two steps: first, we predict stock return using a single factor like news; second, we aggregate all different predictions.

As the first step, we will need a data loader to load news. Next, we need to figure out an algorithm to turn the text news into a vector whose values are the money we want to invest in each stock. If we predict the stock price will rise, we invest more in it; otherwise, we short more of it. The computer algorithm used to do this prediction is the so-called alpha.

In the previous example, suppose our algorithm gets the following value:

$$\text{Alpha (GOOG)} = 2$$
$$\text{Alpha (AAPL)} = -1$$

The values above are a ratio of 2 to -1. This means we want to hold twice as much of GOOG as we do of AAPL, and the positive sign means we want to hold a long position, while the negative sign means we want to hold a short position. Thus, using \$1M of capital as an example, we want to long \$1M of GOOG, and short \$-0.5M of AAPL at the end of today's trading. This example, of course, assumes zero transaction costs.

So the alpha model is actually an algorithm that transforms input data (price/volume, news, fundamental, etc.) into a vector, which is proportional to the money we want to hold in each instrument.

$$\text{Alpha (input data)} \rightarrow \text{alpha value vector}$$

Now that we understand what an alpha means, let's write our first alpha.

We will introduce more concepts along the way.

Above all, we need to define a universe, i.e. the set of financial instruments that we want to build the alpha model with. Let's focus on the US equity market. There are different ways to do this, like using components of the S&P 500 index, using the most liquid 3,000 stocks, etc. Suppose we use the most liquid 3,000 stocks in the US as our research universe, call it TOP3000.

Next, we need an idea to predict the stock price. Behavioral finance states that, on the short-term horizon, the stock price tends to revert back due to the overreaction of the traders. How do we implement this idea? There are many ways to do it. For the purpose of demonstration, we will try a very simple implementation:

Alpha1 = -(close (today) - close (5_days_ago)) /close (5_days_ago)

This implementation means we assume the stock price will revert back to its price five days ago. If today's price is lower than the price of five days ago, we want to long the stock and vice versa. We use the five days' return as the amount of the money we want to hold. This means if the discrepancy is bigger in terms of return, we predict the reversion will be higher.

Now we get our first alpha, it's really simple.

To test if this idea works, we need a simulator to do backtesting. We can use WebSim™ for this purpose.

Using WebSim™, we get the sample results for this alpha as shown in Figure 6.1.

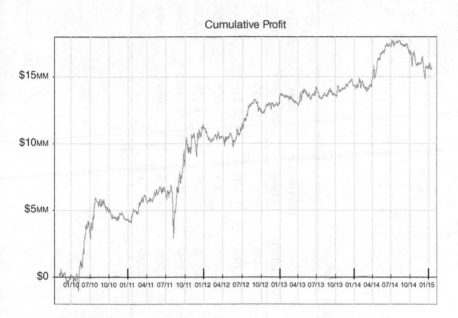

Figure 6.1   Sample simulation result of Alpha1 by WebSim™

There are some new concepts in Table 6.1, as shown on the following page. We list the most important ones we need to learn in order to evaluate an alpha.

The backtesting is done from 2010 to 2015, so each row of the output lists the annual performance of that year. The total simulation booksize is always fixed to $20M; PnL is annual PnL.

Annual return is defined as:

$$Ann\_return: = ann\_pnl/(booksize/2)$$

Table 6.1 Evaluation of Alpha1 simulation graph

Year	Booksize	PnL	Ann. return	Information ratio	Max drawdown	% profitable days	Daily turnover	Profit per $ traded
2010	2.0E7	4.27E6	46.44%	1.32	16.63%	46.52%	62.69%	0.15 ¢
2011	2.0E7	6.93E6	68.70%	1.42	39.22%	50.79%	64.72%	0.21 ¢
2012	2.0E7	2.01E6	20.08%	0.96	14.66%	51.20%	63.36%	0.06 ¢
2013	2.0E7	1.04E6	10.34%	0.60	9.22%	46.83%	63.26%	0.03 ¢
2014	2.0E7	1.48E6	14.72%	0.61	28.67%	51.19%	62.36%	0.05 ¢
2015	2.0E7	−158.21E3	−32.96%	−1.38	4.65%	41.67%	64.34%	−0.10 ¢
2010 – 2015	2.0E7	15.57E6	31.20%	1.00	39.22%	49.28%	63.30%	0.10 ¢

Note: provided for illustrative purposes only

It measures the profitability of the alpha. Information ratio is the single most important metric we will look at. It's defined as:

Information_ratio: = (average daily return)/(daily volatility) * sqrt (256)

It measures the information in the alpha, which roughly means the stability of the alpha's profitability; the higher the better. Max drawdown measures the loss from highest PnL point to lowest PnL point in percentage of booksize/2. Percent profitable measures the percentage of positive days in each year. Daily turnover measures how fast you rebalance your portfolio, and is defined as:

Daily_turnover: = (average dollars traded each day)/booksize

Profit per $ traded measures how much you made for each dollar you traded, and is defined as:

Profit_per_$_traded: = pnl/total_traded_dollar

For this alpha, the total information ratio is about 1 with a high return of about 30%, with a very high max drawdown of 39%. This means the risk is very high, so the PnL is not very stable. To reduce the max drawdown, we need to remove some risks. We can achieve this by using some risk neutralization techniques. Industry risk and market risk are the biggest risks for the equity market. We can remove them partially by requiring our portfolios to be always long/short balanced within each industry.

So basically, we adjust our alpha by requiring:

Alpha2 = Alpha1

Sum (Alpha2 value within same industry) = 0

By doing this, we get a new sample result as seen in Figure 6.2.

As can be seen in Table 6.2, the information ratio is increased to 1.4, return is decreased to 10%, but max drawdown is decreased significantly to only 9%. This is a big improvement!

To further improve the alpha, we noticed that the magnitude of our alpha is five days' return, which is not very accurate as a predictor. Maybe the relative size is more accurate as a predictor. So we next introduce

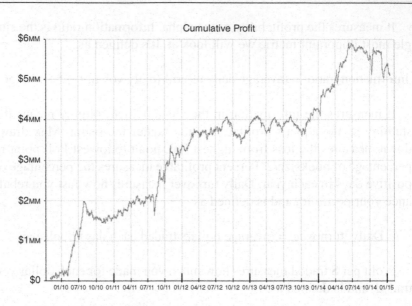

Figure 6.2   Sample simulation result of Alpha2 by WebSim™

the concept of rank. Rank means using the relative rank of the alpha value as the new alpha.

$$Alpha3 = rank\ (Alpha1)$$
$$Sum\ (Alpha3\ value\ within\ same\ industry) = 0$$

The results are reflected in Figure 6.3.

As can be seen in Table 6.3, we get another significant improvement! Now performance looks much better, yet turnover is still a little high. We can try to decrease it by using decay. Decay means averaging your alpha signal within a time window.

Basically, it means:

$$New\_alpha = new\_alpha + weighted\_old\_alpha$$

By trying three days' decay in WebSim™, we get the chart as seen in Figure 6.4.

Table 6.4 looks great! Not only is turnover decreased, but information ratio, return, and drawdown are also improved!

Table 6.2 Evaluation of Alpha2 simulation graph

Year	Booksize	PnL	Ann. return	Information ratio	Max drawdown	% profitable days	Daily turnover	Profit per $ traded
2010	2.0E7	1.59E6	17.30%	2.44	5.44%	51.30%	63.73%	0.05 ¢
2011	2.0E7	1.66E6	16.50%	1.81	5.27%	49.21%	63.85%	0.05 ¢
2012	2.0E7	518.24E3	5.18%	0.90	6.66%	55.20%	63.12%	0.02 ¢
2013	2.0E7	450.88E3	4.47%	0.80	4.97%	51.59%	62.99%	0.01 ¢
2014	2.0E7	1.11E6	11.02%	1.24	8.73%	53.17%	62.86%	0.04 ¢
2015	2.0E7	−231.40E3	−48.21%	−5.96	2.88%	33.33%	62.30%	−0.15 ¢
2010–2015	2.0E7	5.10E6	10.22%	1.37	8.73%	51.92%	63.29%	0.03 ¢

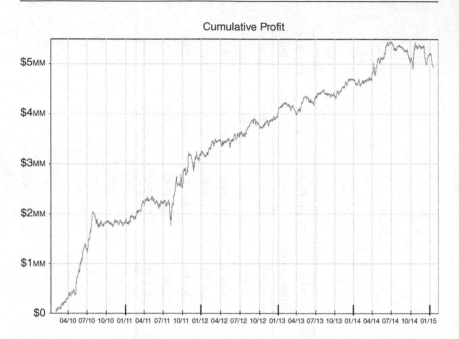

Figure 6.3 Sample simulation result of Alpha3 by WebSim™

We now know how to turn an alpha idea into an algorithm, and learned some techniques to improve it. You can think of more ways to improve it, just be creative.

This is basically how alpha research is done.[1]

The next step is to explore other ideas and data sets, hunting for something really unique. A unique idea is good since you can trade it before others do, potentially leading to more profit.

Good luck!

---

[1] The sample alphas and returns described are included for illustrative purposes only and are not intended to be indicative of any strategy utilized by WorldQuant or its affiliates.

Table 6.3 Evaluation of Alpha3 simulation result

Year	Booksize	PnL	Ann. return	Information ratio	Max drawdown	% profitable days	Daily turnover	Profit per $ traded
2010	2.0E7	1.83E6	19.94%	3.43	3.11%	56.52%	59.43%	0.07 ¢
2011	2.0E7	1.34E6	13.30%	1.70	5.82%	53.17%	59.49%	0.04 ¢
2012	2.0E7	801.74E3	8.02%	1.89	1.93%	55.20%	58.94%	0.03 ¢
2013	2.0E7	692.73E3	6.87%	1.94	2.49%	53.57%	58.69%	0.02 ¢
2014	2.0E7	518.06E3	5.14%	0.93	5.43%	52.38%	59.20%	0.02 ¢
2015	2.0E7	−251.40E3	−52.37%	−10.45	2.78%	33.33%	59.59%	−0.18 ¢
2010 – 2015	2.0E7	4.94E6	9.89%	1.76	5.82%	53.93%	59.15%	0.03 ¢

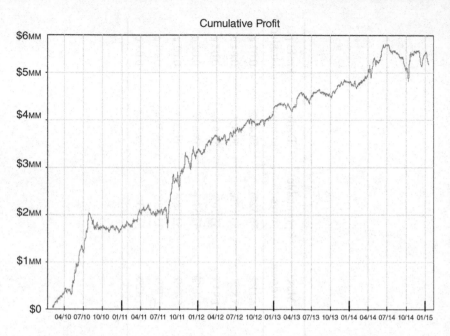

Figure 6.4   Sample simulation result of New_alpha by WebSim™

Table 6.4 Evaluation of New_alpha simulation result

Year	Booksize	PnL	Ann. return	Information ratio	Max drawdown	% profitable days	Daily turnover	Profit per $ traded
2010	2.0E7	1.72E6	18.66%	3.09	4.11%	53.91%	42.48%	0.09 ¢
2011	2.0E7	1.61E6	15.94%	2.01	4.87%	51.19%	42.28%	0.08 ¢
2012	2.0E7	814.03E3	8.14%	1.90	2.05%	57.20%	42.09%	0.04 ¢
2013	2.0E7	643.29E3	6.38%	1.88	2.48%	54.76%	41.87%	0.03 ¢
2014	2.0E7	599.21E3	5.94%	1.03	7.74%	51.59%	42.09%	0.03 ¢
2015	2.0E7	−194.34E3	−40.49%	−7.20	2.58%	33.33%	41.82%	−0.19 ¢
2010 – 2015	2.0E7	5.19E6	10.39%	1.82	7.74%	53.53%	42.15%	0.05 ¢

7
Fundamental Analysis
By Xinye Tang/Kailin Qi

In our alpha research, researchers are attempting to find any strategy that has statistically significant predictive power on asset returns. These strategies, or what we call "signals," are designed by using such tools as mean-reversion, lead-lag effect, momentum, analyst rating information, news sentiment, etc. Fundamental analysis, regarded as the cornerstone of investment, is obviously a very important direction of alpha signal design.

When talking about stocks, fundamental analysis is defined as the technique that attempts to determine a security's intrinsic value by analyzing underlying factors that may affect a company's actual business and its future prospects. We are trying, via fundamental analysis, to answer such questions as: Is the company's revenue steadily growing? How is the company's debt solvency capacity? Does the company have good profitability as well as high earning quality? Does the company have enough liquid assets compared to liabilities, etc.?

On a broader scale, fundamental analysis refers to the analysis of the economic well-being of a financial entity as opposed to its price movements exclusively. One can perform the analysis on sectors/industries or even the economy as a whole instead of single stocks. Contrary to fundamental analysis, technical analysis – which is another major form of security analysis and an important direction in alpha research – focuses solely on the price and volume movements of securities without caring much about the fundamentals of the underlying factors.

The various fundamental factors could be either qualitative or quantitative. In alpha research, we are primarily looking at quantitative factors, which could be measured or expressed in numerical terms. As financial statements are the standard medium by which a company discloses information regarding its financial performance, we often use the quantitative information extracted from financial statements to design alpha signals. Much empirical accounting research has also attempted to discover value-relevant accounting attributes from financial statements in order to enhance fundamental analysis.

Main sources of financial statements are the balance sheet, income statement, and the statement of cash flows. The balance sheet, as a static statement, shows a "snapshot" of an organization at a particular point in time while items from the income statement and the cash flow statement measure the flows over a period of time. It provides a list of a firm's assets and liabilities, as well as the difference between them, shareholders' equity, which is the net worth of the firm. Debt level as well as relevant financial ratios such as debt-to-equity ratio, quick ratio, and current ratio could be derived from the balance sheet. This helps an investor understand the company's debt interest payment, credit rating, and performance with industry average. Other red flags such as large decrease in reserve accounts, increase in inventory, or big increase in accounts receivable also could be exposed in the balance sheet. The income statement provides a measure of profitability over a period of time, where all earnings/profits and expenses/costs data could be looked at. Earnings before interest measure the operation profitability, subtracting any interest burden attributable to debt financing. Due to conservatism, expense items might also include some costs that are not directly related to goods sold during the current period, while some research and development expenditure might not be shown. Items from the statement of cash flow reports important components on the well-being of a firm since it shows the cash change during the year. If the statement shows the firm is not able to meet its dividends' demand but is keeping the productivity of its capital stock out of cash flow from operations, or the amount of cash flow from operations is lower than that from investing, we could see a debt problem – which might be a serious warning.

In-depth analysis of financial statements gives us insight into a company's current and future performance. For example, you may discover, if you study the accrual of earnings in several respects, it has perhaps been manipulated and gives a biased illustration of a company's status. High earnings today could always be viewed as an indication for investors to expect high earnings tomorrow. And the earnings of a company is made up of two parts: the actual cash flow, which is generated from the company's operation, and the accruals, which is calculated and decided by accountants, and thus leaves room for manipulation. To analyze the quality of accrual, it is worthwhile to look at a case study conducted by Sloan *et al.* (2011).

1. First, Sloan scaled earnings, accruals, and cash flow by total assets to compare firms of different sizes.
2. Second, Sloan analyzed the relationship between earnings and quality of accruals. The data used was accruals, earnings, and cash flows from sample firms, and ranked on earnings. Sloan assigned firm-years into deciles based on the rank of earnings, and calculated the average value of earnings in each decile. Then he tracked the results of earnings for the previous and following five years around the calculated year.
3. Third, he compared the results with a ranked one: ranking the value on accrual part of earnings.

The result shows that, when using the earnings to make a prediction, a firm is expected to continue to have high earnings performance for several years into the future if it has high earnings performance this year. But after ranking the accrual component, the power of earnings' predictability performs worse. So we could see that the component of cash flow is much more powerful than the accruals. In other words, when analyzing the future level of earnings, it is more reliable to rely on earnings generated from cash flows, rather than on the accruals.

In order to gain some understanding of a company's value and financial performance, we analyze the valuation ratios, which are mathematical calculations using figures mainly from the financial statements. Some of the most well-known valuation ratios are price-to-earnings and price-to-book. Some empirical research indicates that factors related to contemporaneous changes in many financial statement ratios can yield significant abnormal returns.

Besides the generic items from financial statements, any correlative information outside the format is submitted in the form of a footnote. Footnotes are informative and disclose critically important content to help investors get a better view of the company and make informed decisions. Detail on matters such as accounting policy, changes in accounting methods, long-term purchase commitments, pending or imminent litigation, and executives' stock options can be found. Barely does any company expose its mistakes or difficulties in headlines or tables; hence reading between the lines of these disclosures gives the diligent investors an advantage. In some cases, financial disclosures are used by companies to hide the fact and the effect of changing accounting rules, which might hurt stock prices. Empirically, when there are quite a lot of new footnotes in financial reports, some red flags might be buried in the long paragraphs. Also if you get no revelations from reading these footnotes, chances are that the company is being intentionally obscure. Having the ability to detect early warning signs in the footnotes of the financial reports sets apart the elite investors from the average ones.

We also see quarterly conference calls as a tool for corporate disclosure. While the financial statements give a snapshot of the company's past performance, the conference call gives investors an idea of the current situation and the expectation of future performance from management teams simultaneously. Some commentators would say that from the tone and the manner of the CEO and CFO, especially in the Q&A part of the conference call when explaining the significant deviations in performance with previous estimates, one can gather critical information for long-term models as well as technical indicators. Empirical evidence shows that the sentiment of the conference call can reflect earnings surprises in the following 60 trading days. Also some particular macro-economic variables could be used as powerful stock price indicators in the relevant industry, such as the correlated relationship between the oil price and the stock price in the transportation industry.

Analyst reports produced by the investment bank or stock brokerage, the "sell side," are other informative sources. Since these reports integrate, analyze, predict, and build valuation models via past, fundamental information on a specific stock and the relevant industry, their projections, comments, ratings, and recommendations produce meaningful components. And since large institutional investors who can move the markets because of the volume of assets they manage, refer to analysts' views, these messages are those that you do not want to pass up.

Compared with other alpha signals like price–volume-based signals, due to the low update frequency nature of fundamental data, fundamental alpha signals have lower trading turnover and lower stock coverage. On the other hand, fundamental information tends to be reflected in stock prices over a relatively longer period of time. The cumulative returns to the fundamental signals usually concentrate around the subsequent earnings announcement, and level off one year after the signal's disclosure, indicating a large percentage of abnormal returns can be attributed to previous years' earnings changes of the companies.

Fundamental analysis can also give us ideas on alternative stock classifications. For example, stocks can be labeled as either "value" or "growth," based on the company's financial performance. "Value" stocks refer to those at relatively low prices, as indicated by low price-to-earnings, price-to-book, and price-to-sales ratios, and high dividend yields, while "growth" stocks refer to just the opposite – high price-to-earnings, price-to-book, and price-to-sales ratios, and low dividend yields. Similarly, one can also generate classifications by using other fundamental factors differentiating one type of stock from another. These kinds of classifications, which are related to fundamental information about companies, allow one to better observe market behavior of different groups of stocks, and thus design better alpha signals.

8
Equity Price and Volume
By Cong Li

In finance, the efficient-market hypothesis (EMH) asserts that financial markets are "information efficient." As a result, with the information available at the time when the investment is made, one cannot consistently achieve returns in excess of average market returns on a risk-adjusted basis.

There are three major versions of EMH: the "weak," the "semi-strong," and the "strong." The "weak" hypothesis states that prices on traded assets (e.g. stocks, bonds, or property) already reflect all past available public information; the "semi-strong" hypothesis claims that all past publicly available information and current public information is already priced into securities; and the "strong" hypothesis states that all public information, and even private information, is reflected in a security's price. Thus, given only the current and historical price/volume data, the belief is that we can't realize any profit in an efficient market, and that there are no such things as "price/volume alphas."

Is this true? No, it is not. Actually, with the development of information technology, information processing, automatic trading, etc., the market is already close to, but never at, full efficiency. Quantitative traders seek to profit from those inefficiencies.

Just how can we arbitrage from these inefficiencies?

Information ratio (IR) (defined as mean [daily_pnl]/std[daily_pnl], a measure of the risk-adjusted return of a financial security, or a portfolio) is proportional to the square root of asset number we trade: IR = IC * sqrt(breadth), and it means that, given the same IC (information coefficient, defined as the correlation of predicted return and realized return), we believe better risk-adjusted profit can be achieved.

Unlike some long-term investors who balance their position once a quarter, active portfolio managers typically trade more frequently. They rebalance their portfolio daily, in multiple times. The more often they trade, the more likely the statistical metrics will show. When we add N Gaussian or normal distributions, the common occurring continuous probability distributions that tell the probability that any real observation will fall between any two real limits, and which are independent and identically distributed, the result yields to the same mean but 1/sqrt(N) standard deviation compared to the original distribution. Given the same IC, traded four more times, we can expect two times better IR.

If we look at it from a different angle, given a large pool of assets traded, it's possible to treat them as a whole instead of as individual stocks. If we look at a single instrument, we can see technical indicators like moving average convergence divergence, which is the momentum indicator that shows the relationship between two moving averages of prices, or average true range, which is a measure of volatility that is a moving average over the course of 14 days – generally. When we look at a portfolio, we see different things, such as inner relationships of the instruments, the co-movement as a group, and the relatively different yet weird behavior of a stock as compared with that of others. By looking at the whole group, global optimization and group risk neutralization can be achieved.

Most importantly, we should trade with models others don't have. In this industry, each trader cherishes his or her models very much and keeps them well hidden. A model is valuable only when it has limited exposure. Once it becomes public, the model's predictive power diminishes, and will soon disappear for good. The market is also evolving; the old models decay as the new ones emerge. Consistently looking for new models is the key to why some firms can survive in this business. The models and ideas come from everywhere: they can be inspired by some academic paper, can be our insights on the market, or a flashing thought when you are taking a shower. The micro-structure of the stock price is interesting. That makes us ask: based on what condition does this stock tend to go up or down, and what are the factors that would affect the stock's future trend, momentum or reverse? There are many tools to utilize: math and statistics are well known in the equity trading market; pattern recognition and signal processing tools have also been introduced in recent years, which show that there are many ways that simple equity price and volume data can be used in quantitative finance.

9
Turnover
By Pratik Patel

We generally measure the accuracy/quality of an alpha's predictions by metrics such as information ratio (IR) and information coefficient (IC). The IR is the ratio of excess returns above a benchmark to the variability of those returns. It suggests that an alpha with high excess returns and low variability consistently predicts future returns over a given time period. The IC measures the relationship between the predicted and actual values using correlation, and a value of 1.0 suggests great forecasting ability.

While high IR and IC are great, we must not forget that they measure return prediction irrespective of real world constraints; they assume liquidity is endless, trading is free, and there are no other market participants but ourselves. But actual trading strategies must abide by certain constraints, and an alpha that makes predictions correctly and often, but does so with reasonable assumptions about market conditions, will be more easily leveraged.

WHAT IS TURNOVER?

Predictions change as new information becomes available. Whether a stock moved one tick, an analyst revised his recommendation, or a company released earnings, this change in information is a catalyst for trading activity. We measure this trading via turnover: the total value traded divided by the total value held. A company's stock price changes much more often than does a company's earnings per share, and so it follows that an alpha based on price movements (e.g. price reversion) will usually have a higher turnover than an alpha based solely on company fundamentals. As more trading opportunities provide more opportunities to capture return, we find IR or IC to be higher for price reversion alphas than those of fundamental alphas.

DOES THAT MEAN LOWERING TURNOVER WILL RESULT IN LOWER RETURN?

The tradeoff between return and turnover is certainly one that needs to be balanced. Reducing turnover need not always reduce the quality of the prediction, however. Using smoothing methods like linear decay may actually improve performance in sparse signals with very few events. Winsorizing (limiting extreme values) or decaying the data itself may also help in reducing the turnover in cases where high sensitivity to changes in information may be changing predictions unnecessarily. It will ultimately depend on the alpha. Regardless of the end result, understanding how the alpha behaves under various turnovers gives us a sense for its tradability. One would consider an alpha that maintains most of its return to be more easily leveraged compared to an alpha that loses all return after a slight turnover reduction.

HOW DOES LIQUIDITY FACTOR INTO THIS?

Every trade has a cost, both in terms of fees (i.e. commissions paid to the broker or exchange) and the spread cost. Trading cost is the cost incurred in making an economic exchange. When buying a stock, we not only pay a commission to the broker, but we also pay a spread cost. The highest price a buyer is offering for a stock (the bid) is usually below the lowest price a seller is willing to accept (the ask); this is the bid–ask spread. To realize a return, you must sell what you buy and, at any given time, we may buy a stock only at a price higher than what we could sell it for.

We expect this spread cost to be proportional to the liquidity of the universe or market in question. The top 500 most liquid stocks in the US equities market have an average spread of about 5 basis points (bps). In comparison, smaller markets like those in South East Asia may have average spreads as wide as 25–30 bps.[1] The cost of trading is much higher in these markets, increasing the importance of turnover.

As such, understanding the liquidity of the market is helpful when designing alphas, and testing the alpha idea on a variety of universes of instruments is an important step in understanding its potential

---

[1] These are estimates based on our WebSim™ simulation results. For reference only.

tradability. A given level of turnover might be acceptable in the most liquid universes, but become untradable when extended to include less liquid instruments. Or, what works in one country might only work in the most developed markets. For example, an alpha that trades the top 500 most liquid stocks in US equities with X% turnover may be perfectly acceptable. However, when considering a similar alpha on a larger universe with less liquid instruments (e.g. top 3,000 most liquid stocks in the US), or an alpha trading a developing market, it would be wise to evaluate the performance at lower turnovers keeping the cost of trading in mind.

DOES THE ALPHA ITSELF PLAY A ROLE?

Consider two hypothetical alphas that use price and volume data to make a prediction on prices on the following day. Both alphas operate on the same set of instruments, and let us assume both alphas have the same return and IR. The first simply invests in instruments based on their recent volatility while the second invests based on their current market volume.

$$\alpha_1 = std(returns)$$
$$\alpha_2 = log(volume)$$

We see that the first alpha is investing in more volatile instruments, but as high volatility stocks tend to have lower volume, it makes it difficult for a strategy to allocate a large amount of capital to turn those returns into actual profits. The second alpha, on the other hand, is investing in more liquid, large cap instruments, and is likely to be easier to leverage. If we also pretend that volume data is more stable over time relative to volatility, we would expect turnover for the second alpha to be lower, further increasing its appeal.

SO WHAT IS THE RIGHT TURNOVER FOR AN ALPHA?

It's a balancing act. The turnover margin measures how much the alpha actually earns relative to its trading; it is defined as profit divided by total trade value, which is the amount of money being traded. A good turnover is one that maximizes this ratio between the profit/IR and the turnover. But more importantly, the exercise of understanding how the alpha performs across different liquidity sets and under varying turnover levels should give you a certain confidence about the alpha's robustness and tradability. In the end, it's all relative.

10
Backtest – Signal or Overfitting

By Peng Yan

Traditionally, an alpha is defined as the active return from an investment after risk adjustment is applied. In this chapter, alpha means a quantitative model to predict future investment returns.

BACKTEST

The start of an alpha design can be a hypothesis, a paper, a story, an inspiration, or just a random idea.

Ideas Need to be Tested

Similar to academic research, many assumptions are wrong, many trials futile. Only a few of them will be successful. We are human, and market participants are human as well. Humans are different as they have different ideas; only a small portion of those ideas may generate profits consistently in the real environment. At times you will have a strong belief that the model will work, yet after testing, it is proven not true or vice versa.

Asset class prices can be affected by many factors, either directly or indirectly. One idea may affect just one and neglect others.

Simulation and Backtest

We call the process of testing *idea simulation*. There are different simulation methods, such as:

1. Monte Carlo simulation, which simulates the various sources of uncertainty that are affecting instrument values to get the range of resultant outcomes.

2. Pricing model, which calculates asset price (Black-Scholes model is an example of a pricing model for options).
3. Explanation model, which builds models to explain what happened in history.

In our working environment, simulation means backtest. That is, when there is an idea, we apply it with historical data to check the model's performance. The assumption of backtest is: if the idea worked in history, then it is more likely to work in the future. By the same token, a model will not be considered if there are no historical simulation performances.

Backtest results are used for model pre-selection, comparison between different models, and judging alphas' potential values. Backtest results include different measures such as Sharpe ratio, turnover, returns, correlation, etc.

Backtest is just one additional step once we have an idea. Good backtest performance is not sufficient for a profitable strategy. There are many other factors that will affect investment. As a general matter, one should not invest capital solely based on backtest simulation results. Some of the reasons are:

1. Current market is not the same as historical period. Market rules can be changing, as well as investment participants, new theories, new technology.
2. Simulation assumption may not be realistic. In order to get the assets (buy or sell), one may impact the market, and will need to pay transaction cost or commission. Reasonable estimation for those numbers is crucial when evaluating a simulation result.
3. Possible forward-looking bias. If you saw someone following a trend and making a profit, you test a trend follow model, and perhaps you can get a good historical simulation. Without better understanding, you may or may not make profit in future investment.
4. Overfitting. Sometimes one sees good simulation results that can be just random error or noise, but have no prediction power.

Overfitting is the topic of this chapter. The word overfitting comes from the statistical machine learning field and is critical in our backtest framework. The financial market is noisy, and even a very good model may have minimal positive prediction power. In an efficient market hypothesis, it is presumed there is no arbitrage opportunity to make a profit. When you see some good simulation results, you need to be careful when evaluating the overfitting risk of the models.

OVERFITTING

Multiple technologies have been proposed to reduce overfitting risks. For example, 10-fold crosses validation, regularization, and prior probability. Tenfold crosses validation is a process where you break the data into 10 sets of size n/10, train on 9 data sets and test on 1, then repeat 10 times and take the mean accuracy. Regularization, as in statistics and machine learning, is used for model selection to prevent overfitting by penalizing models with extreme parameter values. Prior probability is where an uncertain quantity p is the probability distribution that would express one's uncertainty about p before some evidence is taken into account. Recently there have been some papers on the overfitting issues in the quantitative investment field, e.g. Bailey (2014a), Bailey (2014b), Beaudan (2013), Burns (2006), Harvey *et al.* (2014), Lopez de Prado (2013), Schorfheide and Wolpin (2012).

Overfitting is easy: After trying seven strategy configurations, a researcher is expected to identify at least one two-year long backtest with an annualized Sharpe ratio of over 1, whereas the expected out-of-sample Sharpe ratio is 0. If the researcher tries a large enough number of strategy configurations, a backtest can always be fitted to any desired performance for a fixed sample length. Thus, there is a minimum backtest length that should be required for a given number of trials.

Correlation can cheat: If we have a large number of random time series, the maximum correlation of a new random series can be larger than 0.2 with high probability, which should be zero because they are all random noise.

Financial markets have memory effect: Overfitting history will hurt out-of-sample performances. Trade noise will actually lose money in the real world, due to the transaction cost and market impact when you are trading a big size.

Academic papers have bias: Academic research papers don't report how many times they tried, and don't report their failures. Some models cannot be reproduced by others.

A higher acceptance rule is needed: Numbers of discovered models were increased in the last few years, and will continue to grow. We need a higher standard for alphas, especially for those cross-sectional prediction models.

HOW TO AVOID OVERFITTING

There are some guidelines to reduce the overfitting risk. Some of them are borrowed from the statistical/machine learning field.

Out-of-sample test: In order to test an alpha model, an out-of-sample test needs to be a true out-of-sample test. That is, we build a model, test it daily in a real environment, and monitor how it performs. It's not right if: (1) models are backtested based on recent N years data, then use data of N years before as out of sample, or (2) take a part of instruments, and use the other part as out of sample. In case (1), the recent N years market contains information of older history, so models that worked recently may tend to work in history. In case (2), instruments are correlated – models with good performance in one universe tend to perform in another.

Please note: when the number of out-of-sample alphas is increasing, the out-of-sample test may be biased as well. An alpha can perform randomly well due to luck. Out-of-sample performance on the single alpha level is inadequate.

Increase in sample requirement: Increasing Sharpe ratio, testing the model in a longer history, testing the model in a wider universe – are all helpful to reduce risk of overfitting. In the real world, unfortunately, there are constraints. There is not a systematic way of increasing Sharpe ratio. Either there is no available historical data that's long enough, or the market has changed and history that is too old means nothing. There is no "wider universe" because it's constrained by the number of instruments in the world.

Make the model elegant: Alpha is better if (1) it is simple and easy to understand; (2) it has a good theory or logic behind it, not just empirical discoveries; (3) it can be explained and you can tell the story behind it. For example, alpha = returns may have potential to be a good model, but alpha = returns + delta(volume) does not. The latter would not work because one cannot add two different units (i.e. returns uses dollars, while volume uses a whole number – such as shares).

Parameters and operations: Similar to machine learning models, with fewer parameters, models perform less sensitively to parameter change. This can help reduce overfitting risks. The value of spending time on fitting parameters is small.

These alternative methods can be useful:

Visualization: A graph contains more information than statistical numbers only.

Number of trials: With the same methodology, recording numbers of trials can be helpful for evaluating overfitting risk.

Artificial data: It is useful to test models on some artificial data sets.

Dynamic models:. Learning models dynamically is better than single time static learning.

11
Alpha and Risk Factors
By Peng Wan

In this chapter, we will review alpha hunting practice from a historical perspective. We will go through a few well-studied market "anomalies" and make the point that some alphas evolve to become "hedge fund betas" or risk factors.

Building on Markowitz's earlier work (1952) on a portfolio's "expected returns and variance of returns," Treynor (1962), Sharpe (1964), Lintner (1965), and Mossin (1966) developed the capital asset pricing model (CAPM) in the 1960s. According to CAPM, a stock's expected return is the reward for its bearing of market risk:

Expected return = Risk-free rate + Stock's market beta * Market risk premium

For the purpose of alpha evaluation, we need to filter out this market beta component and focus on what is left. In practice, when we express an alpha as a vector of stock weights, we usually target dollar and beta neutrality.

Since its birth, CAPM has been challenged due to its overly restrictive assumptions and its contradiction to empirical data. On the other hand, its methodology of dissecting stock returns into common risk factors and idiosyncratic risk is widely adopted in both academic research and practice.

In their paper, Fama and French (1992) added two risk premiums, size and value, to explain stock returns. Size effect says smaller stocks tend to outperform larger stocks. Value effect says stocks with higher book-to-market equity carry a positive risk premium in their return. The alternative measurements of value effect include earnings yield, dividend yield, etc.

Amihud and Mendelson (1986) documented the liquidity effect that less liquid stocks have higher expected returns. Liquidity can be measured by bid–ask spread, stock turnover, and trading volume.

Pastor and Stambaugh (2003) focused on market-wide liquidity and measured stocks' sensitivities to the aggregate liquidity as "liquidity beta."

In 1993, Jegadeesh and Titman (1993) documented the stock momentum effect that recent winners tend to outperform recent losers.

These and other well-studied risk factors played important roles in finance theory and practices. In the future, they are expected to continue to drive a large portion on the cross-section of stocks' returns. As a result, any alpha we find may unintentionally load some risk factors. For instance, an unprocessed raw alpha built from news sentiment very likely loads momentum factor because news writers tend to be excited by high-flying stocks, even if the alpha construction does not involve any price information, from which the original momentum factor is built.

These factors may continue to carry positive risk premium in the future. But we need to be aware of a few issues about them in our research process.

- Given the high publicity of these risk factors, their Sharpe ratios cannot be high. Otherwise smart money would pile in until the performance is no longer attractive anymore.
- Some of these risk factors, such as size and liquidity, require a large imbalance of liquidity between the long and short sides of factor expression, which is not desirable in actual trading. It is also a concern for risk management because it would be difficult to liquidate both sides in a balanced way, particularly in the situation of a market crisis.
- These risk factors generally realize higher volatility per dollar size. They may suffer long-term drawdown due to some macro trend. Moreover, there is an industrial trend that some of these risk factors are packaged as "alternative beta" products (Institutional Investor, September 2014), which may increase their volatility in the future. Figure 11.1 shows a long drawdown of a naïve momentum factor caused by the market reversal in 2009.
- The well-studied risk factors are popularly implemented across the quant investment industry. If some large holders suddenly deleverage their holdings, the price impact may be high enough to force others to follow and thus exacerbate the losses. This danger was most vividly demonstrated in the August 2007 "quant crisis." In the three days of August 7, 8, and 9, 2007, according to Khandani and Lo (2007),

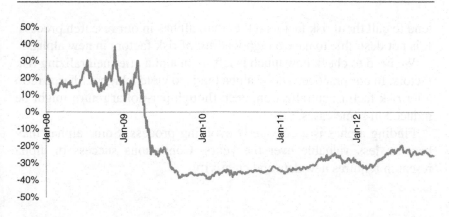

Figure 11.1 Cumulative return of a naïve momentum factor (2008–2012)

popular quant risk factors suffered large losses most likely caused by some players' aggressive unwinding. Thus, it is better to be different from others, and to control the exposure to these common risk factors. Figure 11.2 shows the sudden loss of a hypothetical quant factor during the 2007 "quant crisis."

Therefore, even though these well-studied market effects might continue to generate positive return in the long run (due to either rational risk-rewarding reasons or irrational investor behavioral reasons), we

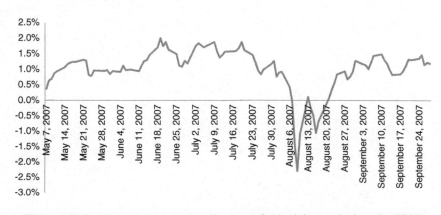

Figure 11.2 Cumulative return of a hypothetical factor during the 2007 quant crisis

tend to call them risk factors rather than alphas in our research process. It is not desirable to have a high loading of risk factors in new alphas.

We need to check how much is left in an alpha after neutralizing risk factors. In our practice, a good alpha tends to yield a higher Sharpe ratio after risk factor neutralization, even though per-dollar return might be reduced in some cases.

Finding alphas is a constantly evolving process. Some alphas may become less valuable over the years. Continuous success of alpha research requires new data and creativity.

12
The Relationship between Alpha and Portfolio Risk

By Ionut Aron

There are many ways to think of what alpha means. Perhaps the most direct way is to think of it as a skill and, by extension, as a yield produced by that skill. Most rational investors seek to obtain the best possible return for a given level of risk. It takes skill to find the optimal strategy to produce that return with high probability and consistency. *Alpha reflects the ability of a manager to enhance the returns of a portfolio without increasing its risk.*[1]

PORTFOLIO RISK

The reference to a *portfolio* in the definition of alpha is not arbitrary. It provides the necessary basis against which alpha is evaluated: we need to know the level of risk and return we started with in order to determine whether the alpha adds value.[2] This implies that alpha is highly context dependent: it may add value to a particular portfolio but not to another.

---

[1] Adding to returns without adding risk does not mean that alpha is a riskless source of returns. Every source of returns has its own risk, but the key is to understand that alpha's returns come from a risk source which is *not already present in the portfolio*. In other words, alpha captures returns from a source that is (ideally) orthogonal to the other risks in the portfolio, and therefore it has a *diversifying* effect on the portfolio risk. True alpha does not leverage the existing risks in the portfolio. It adds a *different* source of risk.

[2] This is not limiting in any way, as the reference portfolio can represent just about anything, for example: an equity index, a bond index, or, in the simplest case, cash.

To understand why this is the case, it helps to think of the reference portfolio in terms of the combination of risks it already contains. Every source of return derives from a source of risk, and so any portfolio can be viewed as a combination of risks, with weights on each risk according to the manager's skill, preferences, and/or constraints.

The difference in performance between two portfolios comes from the number of sources of risk and return they tap into, and the relative weights they place on each source. At one end of the spectrum, we find high-conviction managers, who tend to focus on a limited number of risks and attempt to add value by making larger bets, and compensate for the lack of diversification with more frequent trading. At the other end, we find managers who generally try to avoid market (or factor) timing as much as possible (as well as large bets on a small number of factors), and instead manage risk in their portfolios by tapping into a much larger number of risk sources. In between, there are managers who either prefer a mix of the two styles, or have mandates that restrict what risks they can take, and how much weight they can place on any single source of risk. For example, a manager's mandate could require that his portfolio carries no interest rate risk, in which case he must ensure that the exposure corresponding to the interest risk factor is always zero. This effectively makes his portfolio immune to moves generated by that factor, but it also forces the manager to forego the returns associated with it. To compensate for that loss of return, the manager would either have to take more risk in other factors that are already present in his portfolio, or *generate alpha*.

ALPHA

Many sources of risk are widely known and understood.[3] At the extreme, the manager may be required to remove from his portfolio most (or all) of the known risks (according, for example, to a particular risk model). In order to still be able to produce returns, he would have to research

---

[3] The most well-known risk factors are readily available in commercial risk models. Alpha generally originates from the orthogonal space, that of unknown (or not widely known) risks. However, as a new source of risk becomes widely known, risk models tend to incorporate it, and portfolio construction evolves towards constraining exposure to it, in order to avoid getting hit when that factor gets overcrowded.

and uncover sources of risk that are not yet known to the rest of the market participants, or not yet widely used.

That's what generating alpha means: it is the search for sources of risk and return that are (1) not known to others and (2) different (ideally orthogonal) from the ones that the manager is using already. By being unknown, or less known, the returns from the alpha are likely to erode at a slower rate and therefore provide profits to the one who discovered it for a longer time. By being different, the risk associated with those returns does not leverage some of the existing portfolio risks, but instead it diversifies them. In effect, each alpha provides a new stream of returns and further dilutes the risk loadings of the portfolio (assuming that it is orthogonal to the risks in the portfolio), thus making it less likely that any one of those individual risks would impact the portfolio in a significant way.

It is particularly important to dilute exposure to risk sources that are widely known by other market participants, since those are most susceptible to overcrowding and herding effects, and therefore pose significant risks to the manager's portfolio. A factor poses little risk as long as the rest of the market participants are ignoring it, but once it becomes overcrowded, its risk–return profile changes dramatically. As the amount of capital chasing a particular factor increases, the manager's share of returns from that factor diminishes, while the risk to the portfolio from holding it increases. This is because, at some point, withdrawal of capital from that factor becomes more likely than further infusion, and withdrawals – unless orchestrated by a central bank – have a habit of being precipitate, whereas infusions tend to happen slowly and over a much longer period. And this is precisely what makes it hard to time the exit from a factor, and why portfolios that are concentrated in a few factors tend to have higher volatility than those that are diversified. *Fear drives emotions much faster than greed, so sell-offs happen suddenly, giving the portfolio manager little warning or time to react.*

On the other hand, unknown factors (to the extent that they are *truly* unknown to others) should not require similarly tight exposure constraints, because their risk of overcrowding is presumably not high. Therefore, taking larger exposure to them should be beneficial for the portfolio: the returns are largely not shared with other market participants, and there are fewer actors that could trigger a precipitate sell-off. In practice, however, it is difficult to know exactly who else knows and uses the same alphas, and how much capital runs on them. So it is wise for a portfolio manager to dilute these risks, too. He can achieve that by using *as many distinct alphas as possible*.

LESS BETA, MORE ALPHA

The ideal portfolio (for risk-conscious managers) would therefore consist of zero[4] loadings for any of the widely-known risk factors (beta), and non-zero loadings for as many unknown factors (alphas) as he can discover. The alphas would all be orthogonal to each of the known factors (in order to be truly immune to risks posed by the actions of other market participants), and orthogonal among themselves (for maximum risk diversification inside the portfolio). *The returns of such a portfolio derive only from the alpha component and, to a large extent, are not shared with the rest of the market participants.*

In reality, it is rarely the case that portfolios are constructed with no exposure to known factors. Nor is it the case that factors, known or unknown, are completely orthogonal to each other. A manager's alpha therefore comes from a *combination* of two sources: (1) factor timing (i.e. adjustment of exposures to known risk factors) and (2) tapping into risk sources unknown to the rest of the market participants.

In the first case, the manager's alpha, though possibly unknown to other market participants, is simply a combination of known factors. While such an alpha *does not diversify* the sources of risk of an existing portfolio that already has exposure to those factors, it can enhance the manager's *factor timing*. This allows him to maintain a better combination of risk loadings and thus capture more of the upside and less of the downside of each individual factor. This type of alpha simply reshuffles existing exposures of a portfolio by changing the timing and frequency of rebalancing actions. Even though this may lead to enhanced returns, often accompanied by reduced volatility, one should be mindful that employing this type of alpha comes at a cost. The reason is simple: if the alpha causes an increase in the frequency (and size) of the rebalancing actions, the scalability of the portfolio, as well as the manager's ability to execute that alpha, could be severely limited. In general, the more factor timing a manager engages in, the less he can scale up his portfolio, since frequent (and

---

[4] If the manager has factor timing skills, then non-zero weights on widely known factors are actually desirable, since returns can be magnified by buying factors that are cheap on a relative basis, and selling those that are expensive. A manager with factor timing skills need not search for additional, unknown sources of risk, since he can generate superior returns by simply constructing a portfolio of known risk factors, and dialing exposures up and down according to his timing model.

especially large) transactions can have adverse effects on returns via transaction costs and price impact.

Much more valuable are alphas that do not leverage existing sources of risk, but instead uncover completely new ones, thus acting as *risk diversifiers*. These alphas are (as one would expect) more difficult to find, especially if the number of known risk factors is large (and keeps growing, as can be seen by counting the number of factors in commercial risk models from one year to another). To discover such alphas, one must consciously restrict research to the orthogonal complement of the space spanned by the known risk factors. The process is thus more involved and the throughput smaller. Yet, the rewards are worth it because, besides boosting returns, alphas found this way truly diversify risk in one's portfolio. Their absolute performance, while certainly relevant, is not as important. The true value of such alphas lies in the fact that they uncover a completely *different* source of risk, which in effect adds a stream of returns unrelated to any of the other sources of returns in the portfolio.

THINGS TO REMEMBER

Given the dynamic (and evolving) relationship between alpha and portfolio risk, it is essential for the practitioner who searches for alphas and/ or uses them in portfolio construction to always ask a few key questions about each alpha, in addition to evaluating its performance:

- **Is it truly different?** To diversify risk, the alpha must be orthogonal to widely-known factors, and to other alphas used in the portfolio. Whenever orthogonality is not achieved, the alpha is leveraging existing risks. In such cases, the smaller the overlap with known factors and other alphas, the better. At the very least, the manager should be aware of the overlap, and have a good understanding of how much risk he is taking in each factor.
- **Who doesn't know it?** Attractive risk-adjusted returns come mostly from ideas not known to other market participants. If everybody knows it, it's not an alpha, and a portfolio manager would probably want to have as little exposure to it as possible, if at all. The upside is small, because the alpha's returns (which are not unlimited) have to be divided among all those who employ it. At the same time, the risk

of holding such an alpha in the portfolio increases with the capital and number of market participants chasing its returns, making the downside substantially bigger than the upside.

- **Does it make sense?** If an alpha derives its returns from actions that are inconsistent with the behavior of the market, it is not going to be useful. What good is an alpha that attempts to trade the entire volume of an illiquid asset?
- **Can it scale?** Alphas that rely mostly on factor timing are more difficult to execute, not least because their success depends to a greater extent on the cooperation of other market participants. You need a trading partner in order to execute your alpha. More importantly, your assumptions about his presence and what he is willing to do must be right. The more often this is the case, and the higher the volume you need to trade, the smaller the chances for you to obtain the returns expected from your alpha, since the conditions for you to execute may not always exist, or may not always match your assumptions.
- **Can it last?** A good alpha should be non-intuitive (preferably unappealing) to a first-level thinker, but intuitive and logical to a second-level thinker. This offers time protection against the erosion of its returns by other market participants. A trivial idea is likely to be discovered by others quite fast, turning it from a source of returns with low risk to a source of risk with low returns for your portfolio.

13
Risk and Drawdowns
By Hammad Khan

Risk can be defined in various ways. Measurement of risk of an alpha can simply be done by the level of volatility of its returns and the expected value at risk (which is a measure of maximum potential loss the alpha can incur given a statistical confidence level). Risk can be measured with certainty after the fact. But risk can be anticipated for an alpha with some simple techniques.

- Position concentration in a particular security or a group of securities. For example, in equities, if an alpha takes too many positions in a particular security or a particular sector or industry, we can anticipate that the alpha is taking a high risk if something systematic happens to that security or group of securities. Similarly, in futures, if there are too many positions taken in commodities or bonds or equity indices, there is a systematic risk that an alpha is taking. Such risk can be anticipated by knowing how much exposures an alpha is taking in such positions.
- Some alphas and alpha techniques are very commonly known and are used by many quantitative researchers and portfolio managers around the world. Such alphas – let's call them factors – become a common source of risk because of a lot of money worldwide is riding on them. If performance in such factors degrades, funds may start flowing out of portfolios that are using them, which may cause further degradation in their performance. Any exposures to such factors can be measured by the position and performance correlation between an alpha and such factors, and hence can be anticipated. It may be worthwhile to point out that, in an in-sample period, an alpha may perform very well despite taking these known risks. But as long as an alpha is taking such risks, it is exposed to possible future performance degradation and surges in PnL volatility. Risk is a very vast topic in finance, and many books, papers, and research notes are written on it every

year. Here we have only talked about the idea of risk very briefly in the context of designing alphas within the theme of this book.

Risk of any alpha or portfolio can be reduced by diversification. Having a larger universe of instruments increases diversification as long as position concentration is under control. For example, alphas constructed only on FTSE100 have lower diversification than the alphas constructed on the entire UK and European stocks. However, an important point to note with stock universe diversification is that as we expand the underlying universe, other risks can come into play. Such risks include exposure to various countries and currencies within the same alpha. These risks should be considered, appreciated, and sometimes mitigated by neutralizing. Similarly, using a range of instruments (e.g. futures, equities, bonds, etc.) will increase diversification.

An important point to note with risks is that any good alpha is trying to pick winners and losers to go long and short, respectively. But it will not always work with 100% accuracy. Let's assume that an alpha is able to identify winners and losers, and these stocks continue their winning or losing streak for a long time. If that happens, the alpha gets exposed to a trend in these stocks. Sometimes it may be helpful to have a predetermined profit per trade, after which the alpha decreases the signal in that stock – instead of continuing that streak and eventually incurring a drawdown. Similarly, it is helpful to have a predetermined stop loss per trade in case the trade goes awfully wrong. These techniques are especially important if the universe is not wide enough.

DRAWDOWNS

A drawdown is the percentage loss of an alpha from its peak. For example, if since inception an alpha has made 20% returns and then from its peak it falls down in the next few days (or weeks) to 18% return, the drawdown is measured as 2%. Because every alpha will have up days and down days, there will be drawdowns in every alpha. What we usually concern ourselves with in a backtest are two important features:

• the largest drawdown the alpha has through its history (and in each year of its history);
• the duration of the largest drawdown.

While carrying out a backtest, these drawdowns should be measured in relation to other features of an alpha, e.g. its annualized return and its investment ratio. Sometimes a sudden drawdown can occur in an otherwise good alpha, and then the alpha starts behaving in the same consistent manner. In other cases, drawdowns can be slow and steady negative performance for many days before an alpha starts performing again. Of course, in a real alpha deployment or an out-of-sample test, we would not be able to know whether an alpha has stopped working when negative performance hits, or if this is just a drawdown that the alpha will come out of. Hence, it is important to measure the historic drawdowns in the in-sample period, and the duration of drawdowns. This provides us with a benchmark with which to measure the current performance.

If other measures are taken into account while designing an alpha (e.g. avoiding overfitting), attention should normally be paid to avoiding large drawdowns. The upside should take care of itself. Drawdowns are closely related to risk. Some of the simple techniques used to minimize drawdowns are closely tied to minimizing risk:

- Minimize the maximum exposure taken in any single security.
- Minimize the maximum exposure taken in any similar group of securities.
- Minimize the exposure to any commonly known alpha factors.
- Minimize the exposure to overall market, where the *market* can be a regional or global index, as an example.

While designing alphas, it is tempting to pay too much attention to returns and not that much to drawdowns. But employing simple techniques such as the ones above (and many others not given here), reducing the risks can lead to reduction of possible future drawdowns. You will note that reducing risk exposures will systematically reduce alpha performance as well (because some of the in-sample performance is driven by these very risks).

PERFORMANCE MEASURES FOR RISK AND ANTICIPATING DRAWDOWN

Another important point to note is performance concentration. It may happen that a lot of alpha performance is concentrated within a particular

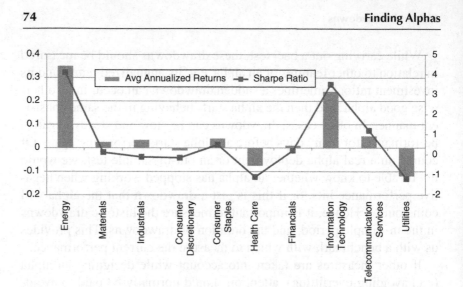

Figure 13.1 Example of an equities alpha where performance is primarily driven by Energy and Information Technology sectors only

group of securities, despite limits on exposures. That could give rise to a potentially risky alpha in some respects. Consider an example: In an equities alpha with limits on sector exposures, most of the performance in an in-sample period comes from just the Energy and Information Technology sectors, and the rest of the sectors do not perform very well.

Figure 13.1 is an example of such an alpha.

Though an overall in-sample performance may look very reasonable, the alpha may degrade and suffer from drawdowns if the alpha stops working on any one of the two sectors above. A good alpha should have its performance distributed across as many securities (or groups such as sectors) as equally as possible.

Figure 13.2 is an example.

This should not, however, be taken as a rule when designing alphas specifically for a particular group of securities (e.g. some alphas are for a narrower universe of some sectors and industries).

Similarly, a researcher should check quintile performance of an alpha. The best way to test that is to divide alphas over quintiles, and find mean (and standard deviation) or returns coming from each quintile. What we expect of a good alpha is that the top quintile (mostly highly positive alphas) gives rise to highly positive future returns, and the bottom quintile (mostly highly negative alphas) gives rise to highly

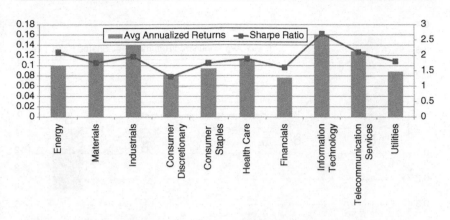

Figure 13.2 Example of an equities alpha where performance across all sectors is not too dissimilar

negative future returns. Other quintiles lie in a decreasing order of performance from the first to the last.

Figure 13.3 shows an example of an alpha quintile performance distribution that is desired.

What we may find in many alphas is that the performance may be coming from just the top or just the bottom quintile, and quintiles 2 to 4 are just noise.

Figure 13.4 is an example of such an alpha.

Because such alphas have good predictive power only in tail cases, the actual breadth of performance decreases and the chances of drawdown

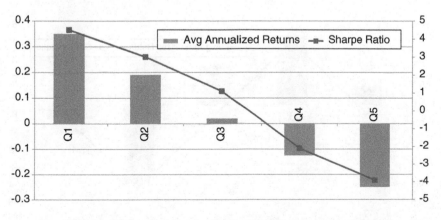

Figure 13.3 A desired quintile distribution of an alpha

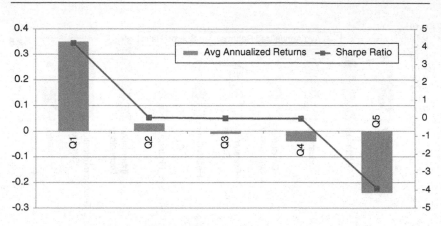

Figure 13.4   A quintile distribution where only tails of the alpha have the
predictive power

increase if the tail information becomes less viable in the future. Since
there's no information in the central quintiles of such alphas, listening
to the central quintiles would not be such a viable option. There are
many examples of alphas that can be used only in tail cases. In some
cases, we may find that the quintiles 2 to 4 systematically outperform
quintile 1, or they systematically underperform quintile 5.

See Figures 13.5 and 13.6 as examples.

Such cases reveal less power of the top (or bottom) quintiles versus other quintiles, and can lead to future degradation in performance
because of lower tail predictive power.

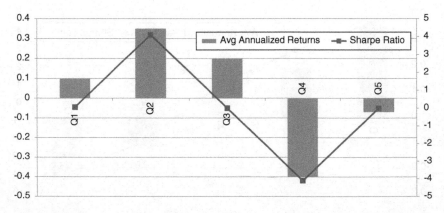

Figure 13.5   A quintile distribution where tails have less predictive power

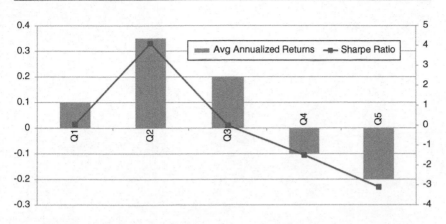

Figure 13.6 A quintile distribution where both second and third quintiles outperform the first quintile

SUMMARY

It is important to consider risks and drawdowns in an alpha design. In-sample performance charts and summary statistics only reveal part of the story of what is going on in an alpha. Correlations with known alpha factors, concentration of performances, and quintile performance distributions, can all help a researcher understand the sources of risk they are taking. While these tools help understand and anticipate the risks an alpha is taking, they can help in a better alpha design so as to enable researchers to reduce future drawdowns by constructing more alphas that adhere to the desired properties mentioned in this chapter.

14
Data and Alpha Design
By Weijia Li

Data plays a central role in alpha design. First, we need the basic data to run a simulation. Basic data means the stock price and volume of a security. No matter what kind of alpha idea you want to backtest, you need these basic data to calculate statistics like return, Sharpe, and turnover, etc. Without these statistics, we will never know if an alpha idea is good or not. Second, data itself can inspire alpha ideas. For example, you can plot the price/volume data for some stocks and check if there is any repeating pattern in history. You can do technical analysis with the price/volume data, etc. If you have access to company earnings data, one natural idea would be to trade stocks based on company earnings.

HOW WE FIND DATA FOR ALPHA

Finding new data has always been a critical skill for an alpha researcher. People always prefer good performance and low correlated alphas. A new dataset can serve both purposes. Sometimes we can get signals from one set of data. The signals may not be strong enough even after we try our best to improve them. Now if we can get another set of data and look at companies from a different angle, we may improve the original signals and make them better. We always want to create uncorrelated alphas to diversify the alpha pool. However, even when the alpha ideas are different, sometimes alpha signals from the same dataset can still be highly correlated. There is an intrinsic correlation between the signals due to the usage of the same data. If we have a new dataset, the ideas inspired by the data set will be new. The way of using the new dataset will be new. Most likely, the alpha signals found in the new dataset will have a low correlation to signals that are based on different data. By using new data, we may achieve both performance improvement and diversification.

Data from Literature

It is nice to have new data to make new alphas. However, how can we get new data? Actually, for this alpha hunting quest, if you find the proper, relevant data, you are half-way through. There are different sources of new data. The most common source is from academic literature. As we mentioned, data is usually associated with alpha ideas. If we search "stock return" on the internet, we will find thousands of papers that are trying to capture the "abnormal return" (i.e. the alpha). In those papers we will learn about all kinds of data used in their studies: price/volume, fundamental, earnings, etc. Once we get the data, of course, we can try the same method in the paper to develop the alpha. You can also acquire some data information by surfing for publicly available content on the internet. However, the less well known the data, the more valuable it can be. If the data is well known and widely available to the public, then many people will have similar alpha models, which will arbitrage the alpha (i.e. abnormal return) away gradually. There still is a possibility that even if the data is popular, no one has applied it to price prediction, so the data still has utility.

Data from Vendors

Data is valuable information, so providing data is also a business. There are lots of data vendors that specialize in collecting, parsing, processing, and delivering data. Sometimes if the data is simple, data vendors may provide only the raw data they collected (e.g. price/volume data). Sometimes vendors can do some parsing and processing before providing the data to their clients. Fundamental data is an example of such data. For unstructured yet sophisticated data such as news, tweets, and so on, vendors would apply natural language processing techniques to analyze the content of the raw data. They will provide machine-readable data to their clients instead of the raw data that is only human readable. Vendors can even sell some alpha models directly. That means the data itself is the output of some alpha models. The clients need only to load the data and trade according to it.

DATA VALIDATION

Whenever we – as alpha researchers – get new data, the first thing we need to do is not to test alpha signals on it, but instead check the data usability. In alpha simulation, data delivery time is a very important factor. For any piece of data, if it is not associated with a timestamp, it is useless. This is because without knowing the time a data point is created, we cannot effectively chart its progression; we would essentially be using the data blindly. Only with the correct timestamp can we do simulation correctly. If we attempt to use the data when it is actually unavailable, we will have forward-looking bias and it will make the alpha performance look amazing. If we do not use the data in time, the alpha performance will not be as good as it should be, and we will be leaving money on the table. For example, if AAPL's earnings exceeded expectations, its stock price would most likely increase, all other things equal, and it would be a good time to buy at the time of such an announcement. If, however, we waited a week to buy AAPL, we would not be able to realize those gains because the "good" news will have already been priced into the stock. So, for every dataset we want to use in alpha research, we need to learn about the data delivery timeline and make sure we only access the data when it is available. As a result, we can make sure we do not have forward-looking bias and get meaningful simulation results. Besides, we need to make sure the data can support alpha production, which means the data will be generated in the future following some time schedule. Sometimes the data producer may cease to generate the data. In this case, the data is not usable for alpha because there is nothing left to provide data in real time for use in the alphas.

Another possible problem with data is survival bias. One example is that one data vendor provides an alpha model that performs well when we test it. This does not mean the alpha model will perform well in the future. The reason is that we do not know how many models the vendor developed, out of which this single model was selected. If the vendor tried 1000 models and only this one survived, we may face survival bias. The bias is introduced by the vendor and is out of our control. In this case, some out-of-sample period for the dataset might be helpful. Out-of-sample (OS) testing is helpful because an alpha that does well in OS testing is a good indicator of an alpha's robustness, since the testing is not in such a controlled universe.

When using data in alpha design, we should always consider a sanity check for data. For historical simulation, one single bad data point can kill the entire alpha signal. In live production, it is very dangerous to assume that the data will always be correct. If the data goes wrong, it can totally distort the alpha signals and cause a big loss. We can do some basic checking, such as removing outliers in the alpha code. With these basic safeguards, our alpha will be more robust.

UNDERSTAND THE DATA BEFORE USING IT

Serious alpha research is based on a deep understanding of the data. We should always try to understand the data so we can make better use of it. For some simple data, just crunching the numbers to make an alpha may be fine. For complicated data, however, a deep understanding will definitely make a difference in alpha research. Sometimes, to understand certain data, we need to acquire some extra knowledge. To understand hundreds of fundamental factors, we need to learn some concepts of corporate finance. Only when we fully understand the data can we come up with alpha ideas that make more sense. Alphas based on a deep understanding of the underlying data will be more robust and more likely to survive.

EMBRACE THE BIG DATA ERA

Nowadays, data grows explosively. Data grows in three areas: variety, volume, and velocity. In old times, maybe only price/volume and fundamental data were considered for predicting stock price movement. Today, we have many more choices. We have so many types of data that we can test wild ideas sometimes. Kamstra *et al.* (2002) present a "SAD" effect (seasonal affective disorder): stock market returns vary seasonally with the length of the day. Hirshleifer and Shumway (2003) found that the morning sunshine at a country's leading stock exchange can predict market index stock returns that day. Preis *et al.* (2013) made use of the Google trend data and beat the market significantly: 326% return vs. 16% return.

There is a huge amount of data being created every day. Take the US equity market, for example: the level 1 tick data is about 50 gigabytes per day. The level 2 tick data is over 100 gigabytes per day. Social media also contributes lots of data. Twitter users send out 58 million tweets on average every day.

Data is also created fast. Now the latency for high-frequency trading firms is single-digit microseconds. People are still trying to buy faster processing and faster connections to do faster trades. Data vendors are also trying their best to push speed to the limit to gain more clients.

More data is always better, as long as we can handle it. It is very challenging to manage the fast growth of data. There may be cost considerations for storage devices, computing machines, customized databases, and so on. On the other hand, if we handle the data well, we have more data to play with. We can make more alphas. We can make faster alphas. We can make better alphas. So, big investment in big data means bigger returns.

15
Statistical Arbitrage, Overfitting, and Alpha Diversity

By Zhuangxi Fang

Can alphas direct the stock market? Or, more specifically, can we predict the price of AAPL on 6/29/2030? Unfortunately, we probably cannot. It is the nature of statistical arbitrage that we can only make the prediction in a "statistical" sense.

The key underlying assumption of statistical arbitrage is that the prices of financial instruments are driven by some consistent rules, which can be discovered from the history and applied to the future. As the prices of securities are driven by multiple rules, each of these driving rules may or may not apply with respect to any particular instrument at any given moment. However, a real price-driving rule, or a good alpha based on this price-driving rule, should appear to be predictive with statistical significance when we apply it to the collection of all investigated securities during all available trading days. A simple example is the well-known mean-reversion rule, which states that a stock's price will tend to move to its average price over time. Within a stock market where this rule holds, it's still easy to find stocks whose prices keep going up or down in some periods, which divert its average price consistently. Yet, if we examine the collection of N stocks in M trading days, you will find more than 50% of these N × M sample points obeying the mean-reverting rule, which enables us to create potentially profitable alphas based on this driving force.

In the quant world, overfitting, or the "discovery" of fake price-driving rules, is a risk that naturally accompanies the seeking of statistical arbitrage alphas. Based on a fake rule, an alpha may appear to be statistically significant in the data history out of which it was developed, but then disappears in the future and never shows up again. An alpha such as "stocks with letter 'C' in their ticker tend to rise on Wednesdays" is probably not a good one to invest in – even if it appears to have been profitable in the past.

This kind of phenomena is also frequently seen in another field closer to our everyday life. A "3964" formula was discovered before the World Cup soccer competition in 2006: Argentina won the championship in 1978 and 1986, which added up to 3964; Germany won it in 1974 and 1990, adding up to 3964 again; there also came Brazil in 1970 and 1994, and Brazil again in 1962 and 2002. Everything looked beautiful, until the "statisticians" tried to apply it to predict the championship in 2006 and claimed that it would go to Brazil who won in 1958 – while it actually went to Italy. Not surprisingly, the "rule" continued to fail in 2010 when Spain became a new member of the champion club. Nevertheless, instead of simply laughing at this alpha, we can still find something sensible from the rule: among all the national teams, those who have won the championship before tend to be more powerful than others, so could have higher chances of winning it again.

This is also inspiring for creating statistical arbitrage alphas. Among the rules or patterns that appear to be statistically significant in the past, those reflecting some price-driving rules are more likely to be predictive in the future. Purely playing numbers like an "athletic statistician" may also help you find some significant results. But in order to create good alphas it's more important to understand the underlying price-driving rule, and use suitable implementations to take advantage of the rule to turn it into alphas.

The prices of financial instruments are driven by multiple factors, such as trading microstructures, fundamental valuation, psychology of investors, and so on. Therefore, it's expected that various kinds of price-driving rules can be discovered to create alphas. Furthermore, based on the same underlying price-driving rule, different alphas can also be created as long as they use different implementation to employ that rule. For example, to take advantage of the mean-reverting rule mentioned above, using different methods to calculate the "mean," and different ways to define the tendency of "reverting," could result in different alphas, all of which may be profitable.

I'd like to use a simple example to conclude this chapter: wheels. Wheels are commonly found to be round in shape. But why do they have to be round? The real restriction for a wheel shape is that it must be a convex, planar one with constant width. So, with this rule in mind, it's feasible to make wheels in shapes other than a round one, as explained by the theory of the Reuleaux Triangle (2014).[1]

---

[1] http://mathworld.wolfram.com/ReuleauxTriangle.html.

16
Techniques for Improving the Robustness of Alphas

By Michael Kozlov[1]

The main goal of alpha research is to predict and outperform the market. However, most investors desire not only returns, but also low risk exposure, predictability of trading results, etc. All these conditions lead us to definitions of a robust alpha.

A robust alpha should have the following properties:

1. Invariance under modification of traded universe: An alpha should reflect a statistical property that is independent of the choice of the traded universe. In other words, we wouldn't like our alpha to depend on some specific instrument or group of instruments. This constraint is frequently imposed by the market as the result of regulatory changes, customer preferences, liquidity decrease, short bans, etc.

2. Robustness to extreme market conditions: An alpha should not have a sharp decline in any of the benchmarks. The most common benchmarks used for alpha performance measurement are information ratio, maximum drawdown, return, etc.

SIMPLE METHODS FOR ROBUSTNESS IMPROVEMENT

We will describe below some useful methods for improving the robustness of an alpha.

---

[1] I am grateful to Andrey Perfilyev, Itay BenDan, and Boris Dvinsky for their comments.

1. Ordering methods
    a. **Ranking**: Ranking is an operation that replaces a vector's elements with their ranks (from 0 to vector_size-1), under some sorting. Usually all vector's elements are also divided by vector_size-1, to be in the interval [0,1]. If two values are the same, they are supposed to have the same rank that equals to the average of their corresponding positions.

    Ranking, for example, can be useful to define the so-called Spearman's rank correlation (Spearman, 1987) that is, in many cases, much more stable than classical Pearson correlation measure (Pearson, 1880s). Pearson correlation is known to be unstable for non-stationary and/or nonlinear inputs.

    b. **Quantiles approximation**: Quantiles are points taken at regular intervals from the cumulative distribution function of a random variable. Splitting ordered data into equal-sized data subsets is the motivation for q-quantities; the quantities are the data values marking the boundaries between consecutive subsets.

    For example, well-known least square regression may be unstable enough for non-stationary and/or nonlinear inputs. However, it can be replaced by least quantiles squares (LQS), for which the target is minimization of some quintile of the squared residuals. The most popular LQS method is median squares minimization.

2. Approximation to normal distribution
    a. **Fisher Transform formula**: Fisher transform is defined as $F(r) =$ arcth(r).

    If $F(r)$ is the Fisher transformation of r, and n is the sample size, then $F(r)$ approximately follows a normal distribution with standard error 1/sqrt(vector_size -3).

    b. **Z-scoring**: Z-scoring of data results in a distribution with zero mean and unit standard deviation. $F(r) = (r - mean(r))/stdev(r)$.

3. Limiting methods
    a. **Truncation**: Limit each stock to be within max percent of total position.

    b. **Winsorizing**: Winsorization is the transformation of statistics by limiting extreme values in the statistical data to reduce the effect of possibly spurious outliers, as argued by Rousseeuw and Leroy (1987).

ADVANCED METHODS FOR ROBUSTNESS IMPROVEMENT

When we try to estimate value from a limited set of data, resampling methods can be very powerful: bootstrapping, cross-validation, etc. For further information one can refer to *Robust Statistics* by Peter J. Huber (2004).

CONCLUSIONS

Robust methods can significantly improve several benchmarks that measure the alpha behavior in extreme market conditions, as argued by Bertsimas *et al.* (2004).

17
Alphas from Automated Search

By Yu Huang

With the development of super-computers and sophisticated statistical models, automating the alpha search becomes possible. Automated alpha search is a method using computer algorithms to find signals out of the huge data cloud. When implemented properly, it can significantly boost the efficiency of alpha search, producing thousands of alphas in a single day. This comes with a price: not all signals found are real alphas. Many of the seemingly great alpha signals found by automated search are noise and don't have any predictive power. Thus, special efforts have to be made in the input preparation, search algorithm, signal testing algorithm, etc., to improve the robustness of these alphas.

In general, there are three components in an automated search: input data, search algorithm, and signal testing (see Figure 17.1).

First, we select a group of meaningful financial data, such as price, earnings, news, etc., as input predictor variables. The predictor variables are usually pre-processed to remove outliers before feeding into the search algorithm. Then we select a target function Y, which represents the future stock returns or its variants. The fitting algorithm then finds the parameters of a group of pre-selected family of functions (the simplest example being the linear functions), which approximate the target function best. At last, the fitted function is tested for robustness.

Search algorithms vary significantly in their search efficiency and search reliability, and there is no algorithm more reliable than most others. However, there are techniques in data preparation and signal testing that will, in general, make the alpha more reliable.

Fitting Algorithm

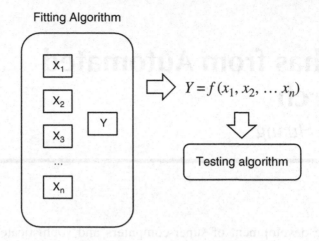

$$Y = f(x_1, x_2, \dots x_n)$$

Testing algorithm

Figure 17.1   Fitting algorithm

IT IS A GOOD IDEA TO MAKE THE INPUT DATA RATIO-LIKE

Good stock returns predictors should be homogeneous and comparable across stocks. As a result, raw financial data such as price or earnings usually doesn't work well as a predictor because it is not comparable among different stocks. For example, earnings data is not cross-section comparable, but earnings divided by revenue is. There are two common methods to make a financial variable ratio-like. The first method is to "compare" the current value of a variable to its historical values. This operation represents the recent change of the variable and very often contains predictive information. The second method is to "compare" a variable with a similar variable of the same category. For example, representing net income as a percentage of revenue makes a comparable variable across stocks.

INPUT DATA SHOULD NOT COME FROM TOO MANY CATEGORIES

It is well known that feeding too many input variables into the fitting algorithm will lead to better in-sample fit, but usually will have worse predictive power due to overfitting. Beyond this point, one often-overlooked issue is the number of data categories. Fitting too many variables will likely lead to an overfitted result, but fitting variables from many different categories is often worse. Here, category refers to the type and source of data. For example, some commonly explored categories include, but are not limited to, price volume, analyst ratings, fundamental data, news, insider trading, etc. Data from each category has its own characteristic frequency. For example, fundamental data usually exhibits clear quarterly cycles, and price volume is uniform, while insider trading data is generally very random. It significantly increases the complexity of the model if the model contains data from many different categories, and the model becomes more susceptible to noise in the data.

IT IS NOT TRUE THAT THE LONGER THE TESTING PERIOD THE BETTER

Increasing the testing period increases the available number of data points, and increases the statistical significance of the result. However, there is an assumption that the underlying dynamics beneath the data are the same. This is not always true for financial markets. The market players and their behaviors change rapidly, which changes the financial market dynamics. Therefore, it is a compromise when choosing the length of input data. If the testing period is too short, we have less data and less confidence in the result. If the testing period is too long, the underlying dynamics might have changed and the result is unreliable.

SENSITIVITY TESTS AND SIGNIFICANCE TESTS ARE IMPORTANT

A good alpha signal should be insensitive to noise. The most common techniques to test the robustness include testing on data from different periods, from different durations, on random subsets of data, on each individual sector of stocks, etc. We have more confidence in the signals that are insensitive to these input changes. On the other hand, each input data should make a significant contribution to the result. The simplest way to test significance is to remove one input variable and check whether the result changes significantly. We trust the signal better if each input variable makes a significant contribution.

18
Algorithms and Special Techniques in Alpha Research

By Sunny Mahajan

Alpha research involves processing vast amounts of raw data. Several algorithms and techniques from engineering disciplines such as machine learning and digital signal processing can be leveraged to extract useful patterns, relationships, and features for alpha generation.

We frequently deal with weak classifiers/predictors in alpha research. The concept of boosting, from machine learning, can be utilized in many cases to create a strong learner out of several weak learners, by learning a suitable weighting function over the weak learners.

Alpha research also involves working with time series data. The concept of filtering, from digital signal processing, is useful in denoising time series data and decomposing time series into trend and cycle components.

Another technique of interest in alpha research is that of feature extraction. Algorithms such as principal component analysis (PCA) help to reduce the dimensionality of the feature space.

Now, let us look at each of these techniques individually to determine their use in generating alpha.

BOOSTING

Boosting is based on the idea of creating a highly accurate prediction rule by combining many relatively weak and inaccurate rules. One of the most widely studied and used boosting algorithms is AdaBoost, as discussed by Freund and Schapire (1999).

AdaBoost learns a strong classifier by combining several weak classifiers using a weighing function, which is learned iteratively. In each iteration, the subsequent weak classifiers are rewarded for classifying correctly those instances that were misclassified by previous classifiers. As long as the performance of each of the individual classifiers is slightly better than random guessing, the final model can be proven to converge to a strong classifier.

DIGITAL FILTERING

Digital filtering involves performing mathematical operations on the raw time series to attenuate or amplify certain characteristics of the signal.

The first and foremost application of digital filtering is smoothing (i.e. suppressing the high-frequency components in the time series). The simplest and most widely used digital filter is the simple moving average. However, smoothing introduces lag, and lag in trading can be extremely unprofitable. As such, alternative filtering techniques can be leveraged to achieve the required level of smoothing with minimum lag.

Another popular application of digital filtering is to decompose the time series into trend and cycle components, as discussed by Mohr (2005). Trend extraction involves suppressing high-frequency components (low-pass filtering), while cycle extraction involves suppressing low-frequency components (high-pass filtering).

A popular and effective filter for low-pass filtering is the Butterworth filter (Butterworth, 1930). High-pass filtering can be accomplished by subtracting the low-pass-filtered time series from the raw time series. Also, low-pass and high-pass frequency filters can be cascaded to select (band pass) or reject (band stop) a specific band of frequencies in the raw time series.

FEATURE EXTRACTION

Feature extraction transforms the data in the high-dimensional space to a space of fewer dimensions. A popular feature extraction algorithm in quantitative finance is PCA.

PCA is an orthogonal linear transformation that transforms the data to express it in terms of new basis vectors – such that these basis vectors explain most of the variance of the original data.

Applications of PCA in alpha research involve finding patterns in data of high dimension, clustering observations (using distance between projections on the new basis as a measure of similarity), principal component regression, and yield curve analysis.

PART III
Extended Topics

19
Impact of News and Social Media on Stock Returns

By Wancheng Zhang

Stocks prices respond to news. In recent years, social media had played a more and more important role in affecting stock prices. However, it is challenging to make alphas with news. As unstructured data often includes text and multimedia content, news cannot be understood directly by computer. This chapter gives an overview on finding alphas by using news and social media.

NEWS

It is not easy for machines to accurately parse and interpret the meaning of the news. Similar to other areas in statistical arbitrage, an algorithm gains advantages in response to speed and coverage, but loses accuracy. Nowadays, trading firms can analyze the news within 1 millisecond and make trading decisions instantly. Big news usually causes large price movement instantly, and sometimes, with overshoot, it reverses later.

Since 2007, the application of sophisticated linguistic analysis of the news and social media has grown from an area of research into mature product solutions. Professional data vendors use sophisticated algorithms to analyze news and deliver the result in real time. News analytics and news sentiment are widely used by both buy-side and sell-side institutions in alpha generation, trading, and risk management.

Sentiment

Simply speaking, sentiment measures the quality of news. The basic sentiment looks at the polarity of the news: good, bad, or neutral. More advanced sentiment analysis can further express more sophisticated emotional details, such as "anger," "surprise," or "beyond expectation."

Construction of news sentiment usually involves natural language processing and statistical/machine learning algorithms (for example, naïve Bayes and supported vector machine).

Sentiment is usually normalized into scores (for example, in range 0–100) to make them cross-sectional comparable. Higher score means news is good, lower score means news is bad, and a score near 50 means the news is neutral. A typical trading strategy could be following the sentiment directly:

If (stock A sentiment > 70) long stock A;
If (stock B sentiment < 30) short stock B;
Use the no-news stocks for neutral.

Sentiment is also useful in risk management. For example, a portfolio manager may directly cut size on stock because of the unexpected news, or estimate the portfolio covariance matrix taking into account the news sentiment score or news frequency.

Individual news sentiment may have exposure to market aggregate sentiment, seasonality, and other timing factors (e.g. before or after the earning season). In relative value strategy, it is useful to compare the relative sentiment.

Novelty

Novelty measures if the news is a brand new story or a successive story of some old news. Vendors may split one long report into several parts. In some other cases, news may be revised several times beyond the initial report. Less novelty news usually has smaller impact on the market, since the information delivered in the previous news may already be reflected in the market. If we view news as events on a time series, novelty is usually inversely proportional to the time-distance between the events.

Relevance

News can have an impact on multiple stocks. Relevance measures the focus of news on specific stocks. Some news is company specific, such as earnings or corporate actions. Relevance of such news is usually high.

Some other news about industry or macro-economics usually has lower relevance to individual stocks. A general news item about the banking industry may affect lots of banking stocks; on the other hand, a news story about Apple's new products may affect Apple and its competitors (like Samsung), with higher relevance on Apple and lower relevance on Samsung. In other words, relevance maps the news to the stocks.

News Categories

Besides classification of news into "good" or "bad," further classification into more detailed categories is also very important for analyzing and making use of news. A category can be as broad as "earnings," which may include all earnings-related reports, like earnings announcements, earnings forecasts, earnings revisions, guidelines, earnings conference calls, and earnings calendars. It can also be more specific, like "corporate legal issues." There are several important aspects of using news categories. First, different categories of news may have different response times on the market. Some categories have longer effects on company valuations, while other categories can cause short-term price fluctuations. Second, markets have different flavors of news at different times. A category rotation strategy can take advantage of such flavors of news styles. Lastly, categories make different types of news easier to use together with other information to create alphas. For example, use the earnings news together with analyst earnings revisions.

"Expected" and "Unexpected" News

A seemingly good piece of news, if the information is already expected by the market and thus reflected by the price, will not cause positive price movement. For example, a piece of news reads: earnings have large growth, 150% compared to 2013. Analyzing this piece of news usually gives positive sentiment. However, if the previous market consensus is that the company will grow 200%, the value in the news is actually below expectations and will cause the price to go down. Therefore, it can be useful to use news together with market consensus and market expectation. Textual analysis and calendar analysis can also be helpful to find out if the news is a "routine update" or "something different." Surprises and unexpected news and events usually result in larger price movement.

Headlines and Full Text

Headlines usually contain the most important information and are well formatted. It is easier to parse and analyze. On the other hand, full text provides more detailed information, but it is harder to work with. One academic research report shows an interesting result: most information in a paragraph is included in the first sentence and last sentence of the paragraph. Similarly, we can give more focus on the first paragraph and last paragraph, first few words or last few words. The paragraph structure and sentence structure can be also interesting to look at.

No News is Good News?

There is an old saying "no news is good news." To some extent, it is true; news means change, events, or something unusual happening. Also, news is usually associated with higher volatility, higher volume, analyst revisions, and more news following up. This brings potential risk to the company. Since more and more firms are using news in risk management, companies that have lots of news might also be cut in size, or even removed out of the investment universe by institutional investors, which can induce lower returns.

News Momentum

If the information in the news is not fully reflected by the market instantly, the stock price may have drift or momentum afterward. The effect is much stronger on smaller stocks, since they are less observed, and on unexpected news. For large stocks and expected news, price reversal after initial overshoot can be observed.

Academic Research

Since 2000, news on stock returns has become a popular topic. Popular research topics cover: aggregation and dispersion of sentiment; "beta" calculations using news; leading news stocks; weighting schemes in textual analysis; news confirmation by day return earnings announcements; the idea that no news is good news; the notion that stocks that are sensitive to news outperform; confirmation of news by trading volume; bias in the news coverage on stocks; momentum, overshoot, and reversal after news; and the relationship of news to analyst revisions.

Related papers can be found by searching "news" and "stock return" on the Social Science Research Network (SSRN).

SOCIAL MEDIA

In April 2013, a Twitter posting by Associated Press claimed there had been an explosion at the White House that injured President Obama. The tweet about the attack was false, however; this Twitter posting caused a huge jump in the market instantly. From 1:08 p.m. to 1:10 p.m., the Dow Jones Industrial Average (DJIA) indices dropped more than 100 points. Just as quickly though, it rebounded in a few minutes. The market losses of $136 billion were experienced within 2 minutes because of one fake Twitter event.

This case clearly shows the broad use of social media in algorithmic trading. Many data vendors are capturing this opportunity as well. Companies like Gnip, which was recently acquired by Twitter, provides millions of social data feeds on a daily basis. They also provide data to third-party vendors who create sentiment products that are being used by many hedge funds.

What Social Media Platforms Matter?

The most popular choice is Twitter, because it can be easily mapped to stock (by checking @ticker). There is also research based on online forums, blogs from professional investors/traders, Facebook, and even Wikipedia.

Academic Research

The first research paper on this topic was "Twitter mood predicts the stock market." The paper argues an accuracy of 87.6% in predicting the daily up and down changes in the closing values of the DJIA. Since then, research was conducted on: the prediction power of various social media; social media applied on individual stocks; the discussion of noise in social media; finding valuable tweets by observing "retweets" and tweets from celebrities; social media sentiment with long-term firm value. Most papers can be found on SSRN as well.

Challenges in Using Social Media in Predictions

Social media is a hot area in quant research. There are several challenges in applying sentiment analysis of social media contents. First, social media has a larger number of records, and updates quickly. Second, social media content is usually casual in format; a Twitter posting can contain a lot of abbreviations and poorly formatted words. This increases the difficulty in language processing. Third, how do we find original and important records? A lot of social media content is in response to some news; these have smaller leads compared to the more "original" social media contents. Hence, there are many fake signals in social media, which is why it is difficult to use social media for predictions.

20
Stock Returns Information from the Stock Options Market

By Swastik Tiwari

In finance, an option is a financial derivative that represents a contract sold by one party (option writer) to another party (option holder), which gives the buyer the right, but not the obligation, to buy or sell an underlying asset or instrument at a specified strike price, on or before a specified date. The seller has the corresponding obligation to fulfill the transaction – that is to sell or buy – if the option holder "exercises" the option. The buyer pays a *premium* to the seller for this right. Call options give the option to buy at a certain price, so the buyer would want the underlying asset to go up in price. Put options give the option to sell at a certain price, so the buyer would want the underlying asset or instrument to go down in price. Speculators use options to take leveraged speculative bets on the underlying, while hedgers use options to reduce the risk of holding an asset.

There are currently 12 options markets in the United States, run by Nasdaq OMX Group, BATS Global Markets, Deutsche Boerse's ISE unit, TMX Group's BOX Options Exchange, Miami International Holdings Inc., Intercontinental Exchange Inc.'s NYSE unit, and CBOE Holdings Inc. Equity options are becoming increasingly popular with both retail and institutional investors.

The Options Clearing Corporation (OCC) in its 2013 annual report presents the following statistics and charts (Figures 20.1–20.3)[1]:

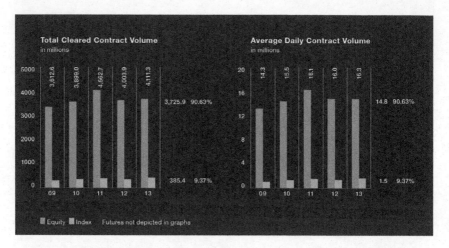

Figure 20.1 Options cleared and daily contract volumes 2009–2013
Source: The Options Clearing Corporation 2013 Annual Report, OCC Chicago, Illinois.
Page 14. Licensed from the Options Clearing Corporation. All Rights Reserved. The
OCC or it's affiliates shall not be responsible for content contained in this book, or
other materials not provided by the OCC. The OCC does not guarantee the accuracy,
adequacy, completeness or availability of information and is not responsible for errors
or omissions or for the results obtained from the use of such information.

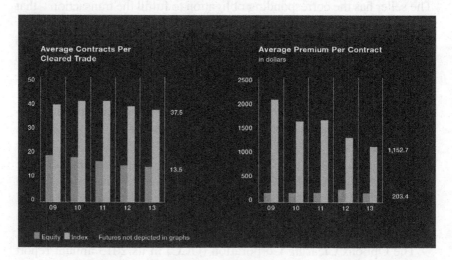

Figure 20.2 Options daily call and put volumes 2009–2013
Source: The Options Clearing Corporation 2013 Annual Report, 86 OCC Chicago, Illinois. Page 14. Licensed from the Options Clearing Corporation. All Rights Reserved.
The OCC or it's affiliates shall not be responsible for content contained in this book,
or other materials not provided by the OCC. The OCC does not guarantee the accuracy, adequacy, completeness or availability of information and is not responsible for
errors or omissions or for the results obtained from the use of such information.

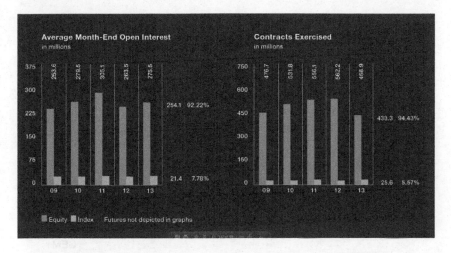

Figure 20.3 Options open interest and contracts exercised 2009–2013
Source: The Options Clearing Corporation 2013 Annual Report, OCC Chicago, Illinois. Page 15. Licensed from the Options Clearing Corporation. All Rights Reserved. The OCC or it's affiliates shall not be responsible for content contained in this book, or other materials not provided by the OCC. The OCC does not guarantee the accuracy, adequacy, completeness or availability of information and is not responsible for errors or omissions or for the results obtained from the use of such information.

OPTIONS VOLUME
OCC TOTAL OPTIONS CONTRACTS 4,111,275,659
Equity 3,725,864,134 90.63%
Index/Other 385,411,525 9.37%

The NASDAQ website[2] in its February 2015 update presents Figure 20.4 on Options Market Share in the US.

The equity options market carries a lot of useful information for predicting stock returns. Equity options contribute to price discovery because they allow traders to better align their strategies with the sign and magnitude of their information. The leverage in equity options, combined with this alignment, creates additional incentives to generate private information. In this way, trades in equity options may provide more refined and precise signals of the underlying asset's value than trades of the asset itself. Understanding how and why equity options affect price discovery is therefore vital to understanding how information comes to be in asset prices.

---

[2] Copyright ©2015 by the Nasdaq OMX Group, Inc. and reproduced by the permission of the Nasdaq OMX Group, Inc.

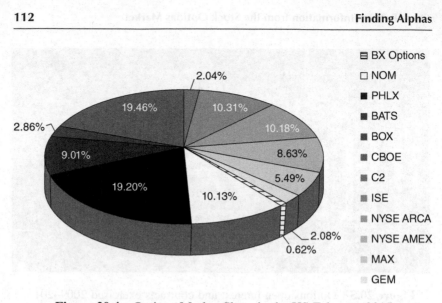

Figure 20.4   Options Market Share in the US February 2015
Source: Chart taken from NasdaqTrader.com, http://www.nasdaqtrader.com/trader.
aspx?id=marketsharenom.

VOLATILITY SKEW

A useful source of such information is the implied volatility of stock
options. Implied volatility of an option contract is that value of the
volatility of the underlying instrument, which, when input in an option
pricing model (such as Black-Scholes), will return a theoretical value
equal to the current market price of the option. In case of equity options,
a plot of implied volatility against the strike price gives a skewed sur-
face. Volatility skew is the difference in implied volatility between out-
of-the-money, at-the-money, and in-the-money options. Volatility skew is
affected by sentiment and the supply/demand relationship, and provides
information on whether fund managers prefer to write calls or puts. In
equity options markets, a skew occurs because money managers usually
prefer to write call options over put options, as can be seen in Figure 20.5.

In their paper "Option Prices Leading Equity Prices: Do Option
Traders Have an Information Advantage," Jin *et al.* (2012) mention the
various past researches in this direction, like Bollen and Whaley (2004),
Garleanu *et al.* (2009), Van Buskirk (2011), Xing *et al.* (2010), and
Bradshaw *et al.* (2010). Bollen and Whaley (2004) and Garleanu *et al.*

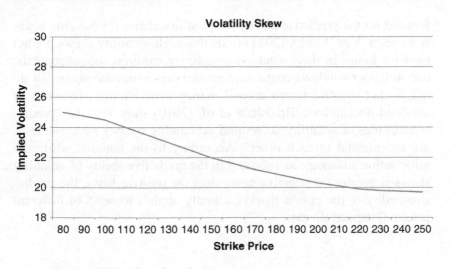

Figure 20.5 Sample volatility skew in equity options markets

(2009) attribute the "shape of observed volatility skew and its predictive ability to the buying pressure due to the information possessed by option traders." Bollen and Whaley (2004) find that "contemporaneous changes in daily implied volatilities are driven by changes in net buying pressure." The option traders with knowledge of positive news create an excess of "buy call" trades and/or "sell put" trades, which causes the prices and implied volatilities of call options, relative to put options, to rise. Similarly, the option traders with knowledge of negative news create an excess of "sell call" trades and/or "buy put" trades, which causes the prices and implied volatilities of put options, relative to call options, to rise. Thus, when option traders obtain information about the possibility of an occurrence of a negative event, the demand for out-of-the-money put options increases relative to the demand for at-the-money call options, thereby increasing the volatility skew. It has been shown by researchers that there is a negative association between volatility skews and returns in the stock market at the firm level. This finding is consistent with the volatility skews reflecting negative information. Xing *et al.* (2010) state that "greater the volatility skew in the traded options of the stock, higher the underperformance." They document the underperformance of underlying stocks of options with higher skews vis-à-vis those of underlying stocks of options with least skews at 10.9% per year on a risk-adjusted basis. There are a few recent studies focused on the predictive ability of volatility skews for extreme negative events. Van Buskirk (2011) finds that high-volatility skews predict negative jumps in short windows containing earnings announcements, and in longer windows containing no earnings announcements, but do not predict negative jumps around management earnings forecasts or dividend declarations. Bradshaw *et al.* (2010) show that the "predictive abilities of volatility skews and accounting opacity for crash risks are incremental to each other." According to the authors, while the information advantage as reflected in the predictive ability of volatility skews is greater for negative news than for positive news, the predictive ability of the option market actually applies to news of different potential impactfullness.

VOLATILITY SPREAD

The call–put parity relation states that, in perfect markets, the following equality holds for European options on non-dividend paying stocks:

$$C - P = S - D.K$$

where C and P are the current call and put prices, respectively, D is the discount factor, K the strike price, and S the spot price. For American options, which allow early exercise, the equation takes the form of an inequality, $S \geq D.K + C - P$. From these relations it can be shown that European call and put options, with the same strike price and maturity date, should have the same implied volatilities, while the American call and put options should have a spread in the implied volatilities ("volatility spread") attributable to the early exercise premium (see Hull, 2008).

However, Ofek *et al.* (2004) document that the "volatility spread" can't entirely be explained by the early exercise premium. Ofek *et al.* (2004) and Cremers and Weinbaum (2010) show that this volatility spread predicts future stock returns. For example, Cremers and Weinbaum (2010) find the outperformance of stocks with high-volatility spreads over those with low-volatility spreads by 50 basis points per week. Bollen and Whaley (2004) and Garleanu *et al.* (2009) attribute the "predictive ability of volatility spreads to the demand-based option models." Higher volatility spreads suggest greater excess demands for call options than for put options, which is indicative of option traders obtaining information about positive news. Thus, volatility spread can be considered as indicative of the nature (positive or negative) and potential impactfullness of the news in possession of the options traders, by capturing the overall net buying pressure in the options market.

OPTIONS TRADING VOLUME

The trading volumes of the options on stocks can also carry useful information about the future stock returns. In their paper, "The Option to Stock Volume Ratio and Future Returns," the authors Johnson and So (2011) focus on the inferences that can be made from trading volumes of options and underlying stocks. The authors provide theoretical and empirical evidence that O/S, the ratio of total option market volume (aggregated across calls and puts) to total equity market volume, is indicative of the private information with the informed traders. The O/S measure was first coined and studied by Roll *et al.* (2009), whose findings suggest that "cross-sectional and time-series variation in O/S may be driven by the trades of informed traders in possession of private information." As an extension of these findings, the authors Johnson and So (2011), in "The Option to Stock Volume Ratio and Future Returns," examine the relationship between O/S and future returns, and find outperformance of low O/S firms over high O/S firms. Their methodology involves sorting firms every month end by O/S and computing the average return of a portfolio consisting of a short position in high O/S stocks and a long position low O/S stocks. They then hold this portfolio for one month. This portfolio provides an average risk-adjusted monthly hedge return of 1.47%. The authors attribute the negative relationship between O/S and future equity returns to short-sale costs in equity markets – due to capital constraints and equity short-sale costs, informed traders prefer to trade options more frequently when in possession of negative news than positive news.

According to the authors, "O/S predicts earnings surprises, standardized unexplained earnings, and abnormal returns at quarterly earnings announcements in the following month." The same O/S measure-based portfolio construction methodology also contains information about future earnings announcements that occur in the month subsequent to the "holding month." They claim that this is consistent with O/S reflecting private information that is incorporated into equity prices when the news became public.

Furthermore, they state that their "model also predicts that O/S is a stronger signal when short-sale costs are high or option leverage is low," all of which they confirm in the data.

OPTIONS OPEN INTEREST

Open interest represents the number of outstanding contracts for an option. In their paper, "Do Option Open-Interest Changes Foreshadow Future Equity Returns?", Fodor *et al.* (2010) examine the relationship between option open-interest changes and future returns. They show that option traders buy relatively more (fewer) call (put) options when they are near term bullish on the underlying asset. Similarly, option traders buy relatively more (fewer) put (call) options when they are near term bearish on the underlying asset. This behavior leads to changes in aggregate open interest having information content about future equity returns. They claim that the informed investors leverage their bullish (bearish) views through increased long call (put) positions.

In their empirical investigation, the authors demonstrate a strong negative relationship between recent changes in aggregate put open-interest levels and the future underlying equity returns. Firms with increases in recent put open interest greatly underperform firms with decrease in put open interest. The authors find that the opposite but much weaker relationship exists in cases of call open-interest changes. They then go on to find the ratio of the recent changes in call open interest to put open interest is the most effective predictor of future equity returns, and that this relationship is positive in the sense that large increases in the ratio are followed by relatively strong future equity returns.

The authors Fodor *et al.* (2010) demonstrate the documented preference of informed traders, as first discussed by Black (1975), to leverage their views through options (bullish views through long call positions and bearish views through long put positions) due to relatively small initial outlay requirements. Fodor *et al.* (2010) present further evidence that the real-world informational differences between the options and equity markets result in differences in the speeds at which information gets incorporated into the prices.

21
Introduction to Momentum Alphas
By Zhiyu Ma

Momentum alphas are an important group and a broad category of alphas. Here we define momentum alphas as average alpha values (the forecasted neutralized stock returns) that share the same signals with a period of past returns (of its own or some other stocks).

In 1993, Jegadeesh and Titman published the first paper on stock price momentum, "Returns to Buying Winners and Selling Losers: Implications for Stock Market Efficiency," which stated that the winners/ losers in the past 3 ~ 12 months are likely to continue to win/lose in the future. Later, many other researchers studied the same phenomenon and confirmed that it works in most stock markets and other financial markets around the world. In recent years, the profit of this alpha has shrunk a lot, and it suffered a large drawdown during the financial crisis of 2008. Then a lot of papers tried to modify the simple rule to enhance the potential profit and reduce the drawdown while keeping the spirit of the alpha. It is still an active field of research within the academic community.

Researchers try to give reasonable explanations as to why momentum alphas work. A well-accepted theory is investors' underreaction to new information. In an imperfectly efficient market, it takes time to resolve and price the new information, as the stock prices gradually reach the target. This holds water when we investigate the impact of events on the markets. There is stock price momentum when public information is announced (e.g. earnings announcements); the more powerful the information, the stronger the momentum effect. An interesting observation is that stock momentum actually starts before the announcement is made (i.e. when the public information was private information).

Not only do investors underreact to the new information, but stock analysts do also. Under peer pressure, the analysts are reluctant to make outstanding (but incorrect) forecasts; instead they tend to gradually adjust their forecasts on future earnings and target prices. So when investors in the market make investment decisions based on analysts' recommendations, the overall decision itself is an underreaction, which explains price momentum effect in another way.

Factor momentum is another type of momentum. In arbitrage pricing theory, we can explain thousands of stock returns by a much smaller set of factors. Stock factor exposure always changes. Yet, when it is compared with a single stock, single factor returns are much more stable (at least over a period of time or market state). Alphas that are based on factor regressions all assume that the factors' returns have momentum effect. Another application of factor momentum is to trade the hot factors that the current market favors by reverse engineering what mutual fund managers are investing.

Another type of momentum is group momentum, which is often related to a phenomenon called co-movement. Related stocks (stocks that are business related, or share similar exposure of a factor that explains returns significantly) tend to move together. When we say they move together, it doesn't mean they move exactly the same amount at the same time. Usually there are a few leaders in the group that move first (possibly driven by new information), and then other stocks within the same group will follow the leaders. This is called lead–lag effect. The lagged stocks enjoy the momentum profits. Besides related stocks, there are also related groups (for example, industries on the supply chain) that transfer one group's return to others.

As mentioned, the first paper discussing momentum does not mention the word "momentum," but mentions "market efficiency." Indeed, momentum effects are related with inefficiency. Developing momentum alphas on liquid universes (which are sets of more efficient stocks) is a challenge, and it requires us to explore the field in a deeper way to find the working alphas.

22
Financial Statement Analysis
By Paul A. Griffin

Companies release financial statements on quarterly and annual time-tables. Securities analysis, popularized by Graham and Dodd (1940), is the in-depth study of these statements on a per-company basis to deduce the potential for excess returns based on the underlying quality of that company. This analysis is used by "fundamental value" investors and hedge funds famously represented by Warren Buffet and Berkshire Hathaway. It contrasts with studying movements and order flow of stock prices, as discussed by Lefevre (1923), or other technical analysis approaches such as momentum-based strategies that make bets based on an expectation that price trends will continue into the future (see Chan *et al.* (1996) and references therein).

Financial statement analysis attempts to systematically measure the effect of factors taken from the earning statements and determine their ability to predict future returns; subsequently, it ranks, sorts, and filters companies to create a portfolio with improved financial strength. (Note that, in this context, the preliminary quarterly announcements and the subsequently filed statements can differ; audited yearly financials are generally considered to be most authoritative.)

The fact that financial statement analysis produces alpha was initially controversial because, in an efficient market, all accessible information is reflected in the market price. However, subsequent works on multiple factors constructed from a diverse and logical selection of earnings information show that violations of the efficient market hypothesis have occurred over long time periods (see, for example, Piotroski (2000), Chan *et al.* (2001), Mohanram (2004), Abarbanell and Bashee (1977), Beneish and Nichols (2009)).

The typical output of traditional financial statement analysis is a stock screen generating a long-only, low-turnover portfolio with a reduced universe of tradable stocks selected by the fundamental characteristics of the corporate earnings.

Modern financial statement analysis is the use of financial statements to weight stock exposure in a quantitative portfolio, which may also be subject to other constraints such as net, beta, and industry neutrality without specifically reducing the universe. In more contemporary terms, one might argue that the factors are predictor inputs to a multifactor regression or machine-learning algorithm.

This chapter is not designed to cover the entire subject of fundamental analysis, as additional data sources associated with market performance, analyst recommendations, and earnings surprises can be combined with the underlying statements to provide additional alpha. A more comprehensive overview is provided in the fundamental analysis chapter of Qi and Tang in this book. This chapter is intended to serve as a basic introduction to the data and can hopefully provide some inspiration for future research directions.

THE BALANCE SHEET

The basic equation of accounting:

$$\text{Total assets} = \text{Liabilities} + \text{Equity}$$

is represented by the balance sheet in Table 22.1.

Note that this statement is for a given date and reflects a snapshot of the well-being of the firm. By comparing snapshots, one can find changes that would cause a repricing of the company's outstanding equity. Total

Table 22.1 The balance sheet equation

Balance sheet YYYYMMDD	
Assets	Liabilities + Equity
Current assets	Current liabilities
Other assets	Long-term debt
Intangible assets (goodwill, etc.)	
Total assets	Shareholder equity

assets is typically used as a normalizing factor to compare factors between companies and also to compare the same company across time. For US companies, it includes the intangible asset known as goodwill, which is defined as what a company pays for another company above book value. While goodwill contains items such as branding, one should generally consider testing if goodwill should be discounted in the definition of normalizing factor.

Some well-known factors constructed from the balance sheet that positively correlated with future returns from 1976 to 1996, as Piotroski (2000) points out, are:

- Increased liquidity (current assets over current liabilities)
- Improved sales over total assets
- No equity issuance
- Less long-term debt

THE INCOME STATEMENT

The income statement updates the balance sheet from one time period to the next, as shown in Table 22.2. Most companies use accrual-based accounting, so the income statement does not reflect the movement of cash, but rather the obligation to be paid. For example, if a company signs a multi-year contract to supply products, it would recognize the revenue when each obligation is fulfilled in the contract, not when the other party transfers cash to an account.

Table 22.2   The income statement

Income statement YYYMMDD	
Net sales (sales)	A
Interest income	B
Cost of goods	C
Operating expenses	D
Income taxes	E
Gross margin	A–C
Income from operations	A–C–D
Gross income	A + B
Net income	A + B – C – D – E

The following factors based on the income statement are positively correlated with futures returns in the US from 1976 to 1996, as according to Piotroski (2000):

- Net income > 0
- Improved net income over total assets
- Improved gross margin

THE CASH FLOW STATEMENT

The cash flow statement, as shown in Table 22.3, describes the sources of the change in cash balance from one period to the next.
Factors positively correlated with future returns in the US from 1976 to 1996 are:

- Cash from operations > 0
- Cash from operations > net income

Table 22.3   The cash flow statement

Cash flow statement YYYMMDD	
Cash balance	A
Cash from operations	B
Borrowings	C
Stock sale	D
Purchases	E
Taxes	F
Cash flow	B + C + D – E – F
Cash balance	A + B + C + D – E – F

GROWTH

The factors above are focused on finding quality in company performance. However, investors may also be interested in growth prospects.

A similar regression analysis for growth stocks was performed by Chan *et al.* (2001) and Mohanram (2004), and they found signals that correlate with future returns specifically for growth stocks (with low book-to-market ratio) from 1979 to 1999:

- Net income/total assets > industry median
- Cash flow/total assets > industry median
- Net income variance < industry median
- Gross income variance < industry median
- R&D expenses/total assets > industry median
- Capital expenditure/total assets > industry median
- Advertising expenses/total assets > industry median

R&D, Capital, and Advertising Expenses are separate items inside the Operating Expenses line item of the Income Statement as indicated in Table 22.4. Growing companies will build out these areas with expectations of improved future sales.

Table 22.4   Income statement: operating expenses

R&D expenses	D1
Capital expenses	D2
Advertising expenses	D3
Other operating expenses	D4
Operating expenses	D = D1 + D2 + D3 + D4

CORPORATE GOVERNANCE

Management monitors and improves company performance using metrics, and market participants will tend to reward the stock price when they observe improvements in some of these. Metrics positively correlated with future returns, according to Abarbanell and Bushee (1997), are:

- Reduced inventory per unit sales
- Improved accounts receivable per unit sales
- Improved sales minus change in gross margin
- Reduced administrative expenses per unit sales
- Improved tax rate

- Earns quality – change to the use of FIFO versus LIFO
- Audit qualification – change to qualified auditing
- Sales per employee

FACTOR ANALYSIS IN NON-US MARKETS

Recent work confirms that factor analysis provides excess return predictions in non-US markets.

Negative Factors

There is some literature specifically useful for isolating a short portfolio. The basic ideas, as pointed out by Beneish and Nichols (2009), are to search for earnings manipulation, a history of mergers, equity issuance, and other forms of management efforts, to improve earnings or cash flow without actually improving the core business.

- Higher net sales than free cash flow
- Low book to price
- High sales growth
- Low cash flow from operations to price
- Acquisition in last five years
- Equity issuance > industry average over two years

High financial leverage, defined as:

- Net financing debt over common equity

is shown by Nissim and Penman (2003) to negatively correlate with operating profitability, where the definition of financial leverage excludes operating liabilities. High long-term or financial debt can be a signal of pending liquidity issues or even insolvency. A well-known case study in the misguided application of financial leverage is the history of the Long-Term Capital Management investment firm. Also, the Enron Corporation accounting scandal was based on the use of special purpose vehicles to keep long-term debt off the balance sheet, and the corrected accounting of debt led to its insolvency. Generally, additional leverage adds risk that can lead to either higher profits or risk of ruin. Therefore, the reader is urged to perform statistical analysis of leverage and debt in conjunction with other factors to determine combinations that indicate meaningful positive or negative correlations with future returns.

Special Considerations

Commodity-based industries have sales affected by the underlying commodity price, so sales increases are not necessarily a measure of improved company performance. Banks have different reporting requirements and should be given special treatment. The phase of the economic cycle may affect the correlation of debt with price appreciation and significantly impact factors closely associated with growth.

Converting Factors to Strategies

The most discussed method in the investment literature to apply factors is by constructing a universe screen, particularly by the mechanism of assigning a score of +1 to a company when it passes a test, then combining scores over all factors, and subsequently taking a long position the highest rated companies. This is generally a reasonable fusion method given ignorance of the results of a more significant statistical analysis, according to Kahneman (2011).

Converting Factors to Alphas

Note that most of the scores are rate-of-change based, and one generally subtracts the latest statement data from the previous year(s), because seasonality will effect direct quarter over quarter comparisons. Statement data may be delayed for alpha analysis, and one should be careful to note the time delays in your data usage for alpha generation. Point-in-time financial data provides significantly more realistic (and worse backtesting) results due to the removal of the forward bias associated with statement refilings.

It may be beneficial to perform your own statistical analysis on factors, possibly with some form of regression. It also might be useful to measure the factor correlations. There is opportunity to employ machine learning techniques such as a genetic algorithm to find good factor combinations, and this may be particularly successful if the inputs are based on a thorough understanding of the meaning of the factors. The market rewards alpha based on new meaningful factor combinations, so researchers should think creatively and perform literature scans for the latest ideas.

23
Institutional Research 101
By Benjamin Ee[1]

This chapter is focused on how alpha researchers can add institutional research sources to their toolkit for generating new trading ideas.

Part 1 provides a "tourist guide" of sorts to the various streams of academic research on financial markets that have been energetically developed over the previous few decades. Part 2 is a general overview of analyst research and stock recommendations that researchers may encounter frequently in financial media. We talk about how to access analyst recommendations, as well as address the all-important question of how they can help to inspire systematic trading ideas.

ACADEMIC RESEARCH ON FINANCIAL MARKETS – NEEDLE MEETS HAYSTACK?

How should you find ideas for new market strategies? Inspiration can come from many sources including discussions with classmates, colleagues or friends, the financial press, seminars, books, and so on. In

[1] The authors of this chapter would like to thank WanCheng Zhang, Zhiyu Ma, Kailin Qi, and KunChing Lin for comments and suggestions. The author makes no warranties, express or implied, concerning the accuracy or completeness of the information presented here within. All information is for educational and informational purposes only.

this chapter, we introduce another source for idea generation that the researcher can add to her toolkit: freely available academic papers on financial markets.

At first glance, the explosion of publicly available finance research by professors, graduate students, various market commentators, and others over the last few decades can make navigating existing works a daunting task for any newcomer. A search for "corporate finance" and "asset pricing" on Google Scholar in December 2014 yielded about 1.5 million and 1.3 million results, respectively; paring down the search to something far more specific, say the "cross-section of stock returns," yields close to 10,000 results, including material from one of the 2014 Nobel Prize laureates.

A digestion of all existing works may therefore not be the best way to get quick inspiration.

This section attempts to provide a "rough and ready" guide for the newcomer to quickly start adding academic papers as a great source of ideas to their toolkit. Papers can be accessed via several means, some of which cost only as much as an internet connection. One important distinction is between "vetted" sources such as journals, and "open" sources.

Journals

Formal academic journals are where professors and professional researchers publish their results. Papers in formal journals have undergone a rigorous peer-review process, where other researchers critique them. Consequently, research that survived this process will usually be free of serious methodological errors. You may be able to get inspiration, not just for trading ideas, but also for new methodologies.

The topics discussed in these publications are usually representative of what the academic community judges to be "important" *at the time of publication*. This may only overlap partially with the priorities of a market strategist. The primary focus of the academic community is not to search for market strategies, but to understand the underlying forces governing economic interactions. There is a significant overlap between the two, but not every paper will be relevant. One easy way to understand the difference is by analogy to similar situations in the physical sciences – e.g. between investigating the fundamental laws of electromagnetism on the one hand, and building an MRI machine on the other.

Papers with conclusions that are more "general" are typically published in journals with a higher impact factor, and these will also be papers that the community pays more attention to. This has pluses and minuses for the strategist who wishes to make use of conclusions in such papers. There will be more work for you to do, going from a discussion on general economic forces such as "moral hazard," to specific strategies. The discussion in journals may be a step removed from markets, and you might need to connect the dots yourself. On the other hand, there could be valuable economic ingredients in these, improving many strategies that you construct. Designing a new strategy by yourself based on inspiration from fundamental forces, as opposed to directly replicating applied findings, also makes it likely that your strategy will be different from other market participants. Table 23.1 shows some "general interest" journals in economics and finance that we have found useful in the past. If you have the time, it would be useful to check some of them out.[2]

Table 23.1 General interest economics and finance journals

Journal	Link	2014 RePec rank (impact factor)
The Quarterly Journal of Economics	qje.oxfordjournals.org	#1 (66)
Econometrica	http://onlinelibrary.wiley.com/journal/10.1111/(ISSN)1468-0262	#3 (57)
Journal of Financial Economics	http://jfe.rochester.edu/	#5 (40)
Journal of Political Economy	http://www.press.uchicago.edu/ucp/journals/journal/jpe.html	#7 (34)
Review of Financial Studies	http://rfs.oxfordjournals.org/	#10 (31)
American Economic Review	https://www.aeaweb.org/aer/index.php	#12 (29)
Journal of Finance	http://www.afajof.org/view/index.html	#15 (25)

If you have time, also check out some of the other top journals in economics and finance at https://www.idea.repec.org/top/top.journals.simple.html.

---

[2] These are usually not free. Apart from paying, also consider your local library, or local university library, which may have subscriptions. Some universities also provide electronic access to alumni free of charge or for a small fee. Lastly, consider emailing the authors directly – you never know!

In contrast with "general interest" journals, there are also "investments focused" journals, where work is more firmly aligned with describing strategies, or methodologies that are directly relevant in finding strategies. In some cases, it is more likely that you will be able to directly code up and replicate the strategy discussed. As mentioned above, the downside is that strategies may be described in such detail that the rest of the world could also be doing this. Nevertheless, once you have the core of a strategy coded up and tested, you can think about using it as a basis for further innovation. This might be easier than starting from square one. Table 23.2 lists some recommendations based on a listing from the CFA Institute.

If academics have viable market strategies, why would they not keep them secret and trade the strategies themselves? Possible responses to this question include:

- One of their objectives could be to demonstrate the plausibility of theories about economic interactions, and the fact that their framework is consistent with market reactions is one of several pieces of evidence.
- **Execution matters**: Developing the infrastructure for efficient execution of otherwise excellent market strategies is a non-trivial undertaking, costly in terms of both time and capital.
- **Career and reputational considerations**: The expected benefit from publishing, e.g. in terms of the intellectual impact to one's field, media mentions, potential consulting contracts, might factor into the decision to share the information.
- **Lag time**: It can take several years for a new academic paper to make it from conception to polished product in a journal. If the paper describes a highly actionable strategy, it will likely already have been picked up and implemented by other market participants in the meantime.
- **Cost**: Academic journals are expensive; you may be able to access these papers via your university/local library, or, in some cases, email the authors directly for a copy. Most academic authors are happy to send out copies of their papers.

Open Sources

These are repositories of papers that are generally free to access and, occasionally, free to contribute to. One implication of the latter feature is that papers may not have gone through the traditional peer-review

Table 23.2 "Investments focused" journals

Journal	Link
Financial Analysts Journal	http://www.cfapubs.org/loi/faj
Financial Management	http://onlinelibrary.wiley.com/journal/10.1111/(ISSN)1755-053X
Financial Review	http://onlinelibrary.wiley.com/journal/10.1111/(ISSN)1540-6288
Journal of Banking and Finance	http://www.journals.elsevier.com/journal-of-banking-and-finance
Journal of Business	http://www.jstor.org/page/journal/jbusiness/about.html
Journal of Corporate Finance	http://www.journals.elsevier.com/journal-of-corporate-finance
Journal of Empirical Finance	http://www.journals.elsevier.com/journal-of-emplrical-finance
Journal of Financial and Quantitative Analysis	http://depts.washington.edu/jfqa
Journal of Financial Intermediation	http://www.journals.elsevier.com/journal-of-financial-intermediation
Journal of Financial Markets	http://www.journals.elsevier.com/journal-of-financial-markets/
Journal of Financial Research	http://onlinelibrary.wiley.com/journal/10.1111/(ISSN)1475-6803
Journal of Futures Markets	http://onlinelibrary.wiley.com/journal/10.1002/(ISSN)1096-9934
Journal of International Money and Finance	http://www.journals.elsevier.com/journal-of-international-money-and-finance/
Journal of Portfolio Management	http://www.iijournals.com/toc/jpm/current
Pacific-Basin Finance Journal	http://www.journals.elsevier.com/pacific-basin-finance-journal
Review of Quantitative Finance and Accounting	http://www.springer.com/business+%26+management/finance/journal/11156

process. In many cases, they may be early versions of formal academic papers, and so are written with the intention of ultimately passing review. Examples of open sources include papers on SSRN or arXiv. Once you have developed your own list of favorite academic authors, also check out the working papers section of their websites.

Table 23.3 lists open sources of papers.
Characteristics of open sources:

- **Lower lag time**: The latest research, by definition, will usually be a working paper rather than a published article. Capacity-limited market strategies are best implemented as soon as possible.
- **Generally free**: Working papers may generally be distributed by their authors for free, and most authors have an incentive to maximize ease of distribution.
- **Greater variety**: Formally reviewed journals represent the priorities of the communities whose work they chronicle. As with all fields, some subareas get greater prominence and discussion from time to time. There is no guarantee the contemporary focus of formal journals will be of the greatest interest to market strategists. However, a broader array of work can be found on SSRN or arXiv, where authors have greater latitude; the downside is that readers need to be more discerning in trying to decide how to spend their time.
- **No peer review (yet)**: No peer review generally means that there is no real guarantee that the paper does not contain serious errors on methodology. Definitely exercise judgment on the subject matter; there are also several simple heuristics one can apply:
  - Has the author published in peer-reviewed papers before?
  - Is the paper intended for peer review (they may say "submitted to XYZ journal" on their website or in footnotes).
  - Are conclusions based on commonly-used datasets (e.g. Compustat, CRSP), or rare/self-collected data. If the authors' findings are based on rare data, is there any way to replicate the essence of their

Table 23.3 "Open" sources

Name	Link
SSRN	http://www.ssrn.com/en
arXiv	http://arxiv.org
NBER website (working papers are only provided free of charge if downloaders meet specified criteria)	http://www.nber.org
CFA Institute website	http://www.cfainstitute.org/learning/tools/Pages/index.aspx

theories using commonly available data? You will usually need to do so in order to create a viable market strategy anyway.

- Is the methodology commonly used and intuitive?

A final source of research papers worth investigating are papers commissioned or released by market data vendors. These are papers that demonstrate viable strategies based primarily on the data being sold by the company in question (e.g. CRSP, WRDS, etc.), and therefore serve a marketing purpose, at least in part. Nonetheless, these can help you get up to speed on a new dataset quickly, and the strategies may also be transferrable. Examples include OptionMetrics (http://www.optionmetrics.com/research.html) and Ravenpack (http://www.ravenpack.com/research/white-papers/).

Following the Debate

One nice thing about publicly-shared research is that it invites debate. Other researchers write follow-up papers to critique and improve upon already published work. Following this debate may be useful if you are trying to figure out how to improve upon an existing framework, or would like to know what most people say about its strengths and weaknesses.

Most academic researchers in a university environment usually know what the community is saying about their latest paper. The same may not apply to you, sitting in your office or at home, reading the latest issue of *Journal of Finance*. How can you find out what other professional researchers are saying about the article you just read?

One way to do so is by following the citations of a paper. Citations are other academic papers that contain references to the paper that you just read. Often, they may discuss improvements, tweaks, or critiques. Contemporary information technology has made it fairly easy to follow these citations. Take any given paper, say "The Cross-Section of Expected Stock Returns" (not an entirely bad starting point for a novice strategist). Entering this into Google Scholar (this is different from regular Google; use http://scholar.google.com), we get Figure 23.1.

Immediately we see that the paper has been cited by more than 10,000 other papers as of December 2014. Clicking on the link that says "Cited by XXX" (highlighted by the black box in the figure), Google Scholar very helpfully returns a listing of papers that make some reference to the aforementioned paper as seen in Figure 23.2.

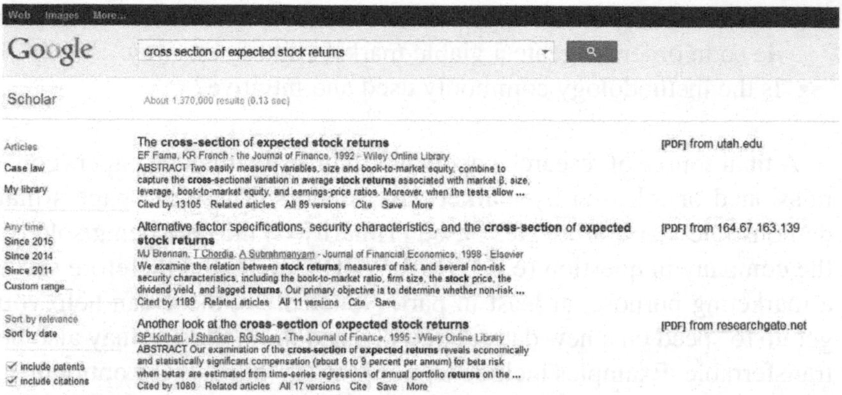

Figure 23.1   The search result of "The Cross-Section of Expected Stock Returns" on Google Scholar
Source: Google and the Google logo are registered trademarks of Google Inc., used with permission.

Following citations is a great way to find out everything that has been said about a given topic, and to figure out what has already been discussed as viable improvements and critiques of published ideas. As they say, no point reinventing the wheel!

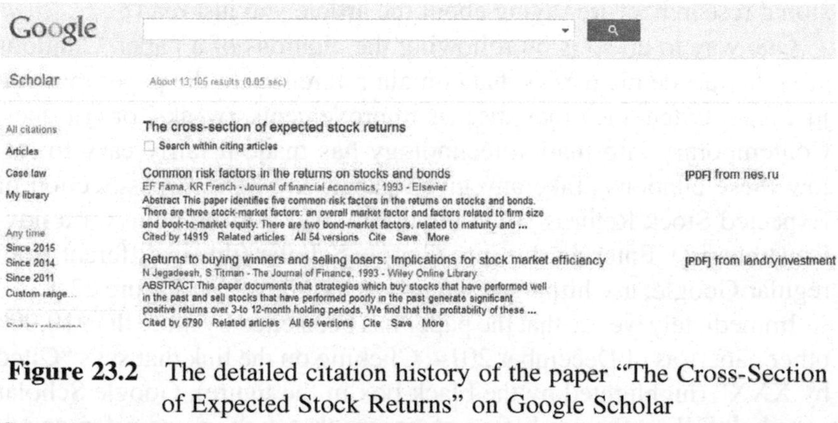

Figure 23.2   The detailed citation history of the paper "The Cross-Section of Expected Stock Returns" on Google Scholar
Source: Google and the Google logo are registered trademarks of Google Inc., used with permission.

Do the Authors of Academic Research Actually Believe Viable Market Strategies are Possible?

Congratulations! You have successfully made it to this part of a chapter discussing academic research, no small accomplishment.

Saving the most difficult questions for last, we may ask:

- Do academic researchers actually think it is possible to write down viable market strategies?
- Why are we even reading what these guys write, anyway, if they do not think that it is possible?

Both are fair questions. If you have any interest at all in markets, you have probably, at some point or another, engaged in debate with your college professors about beating the market. The words "efficient markets hypothesis" (EMH) and "not possible" may even come to mind, and the debate can be frustrating, not in the least because market returns on some days feel like a 10 mph speed limit on the interstate.

I would guess that academic researchers take the EMH so seriously not because it is an unbreakable law to be placed in the same category as the laws of gravity or motion. Rather, it is because market anomalies do, in fact, exist, but they need to be examined, checked, and double checked with extremely great care. On the one hand, market anomalies[3] resulting from a variety of historical, institutional, legal, political, or economic reasons provide opportunities for profit; on the other hand, history is filled with investors who confused market anomalies with risk factors, and paid dearly.

In Summary

- It may be worth adding sources of academic research to your toolkit for finding new ideas.

---

[3] Strictly speaking, the existence of market anomalies (even extreme ones such as true arbitrage opportunities) may not disprove the EMH. "What is the definition of market returns?" If we also include all possible profits from market anomalies into the definition of "market returns," then the EMH remains unchallenged. In any case, to the extent that market anomalies allow us to make more money while controlling risk, the point is academic.

- There have been *countless* papers written in finance research over the last few decades.
- A strategy for navigating these is essential. Established and well-regarded peer-reviewed journals can serve as potential starting points. Grouping papers into "conversation threads" by following citations is another complementary strategy, where you only follow the threads that you are interested in.
- The EMH is not an unbreakable law, but it deserves to be taken seriously.

ANALYST RESEARCH

"Goldman Sachs upgrades Netflix"

– TheStreet.com, July 2014

"Morgan Stanley downgrades technology sector"

– Yahoo Finance, December 2014

"Citigroup maintains rating on Alcoa Inc."

– MarketWatch.com, December 2014

Research by sell-side analysts on firms and entire industries feature prominently in financial newspapers, conferences, blogs, and databases. It is not unusual to see analyst recommendations, upgrades, downgrades, or price target changes feature prominently in explanations of major stock price movements. Numerous studies by industry associations and academics have found that there is, indeed, valuable information contained in analyst research (see Francis *et al.* (2002) and Frankel *et al.* (2006)).

Nevertheless, "stock analyst" conjures up images of sophisticated researchers from Goldman Sachs or JP Morgan conducting high-powered earnings calls with Fortune 500 CEOs to gather information, and then presenting their findings to multibillion-dollar institutional funds. Against this image, how can you, as a new alpha researcher (with slightly less than a few billion dollars at your disposal), access this valuable body of analysis? Just as importantly, why should a researcher who is interested in constructing systematic market strategies be equally interested in what is typically company-specific analysis?

Accessing Analyst Research (for Free, of Course)

One interesting fact about stock analyst research is that some of it is surprisingly accessible, with the financial media acting as a valuable intermediary. "Financial media" in this case includes not only traditional sources like *The Wall Street Journal* or Bloomberg, but also aggregator websites such as Yahoo Finance and Google Finance. The latter are particularly useful in looking up analyst analysis, estimates, or questions during earning calls. As with academic research, most of these websites have at least some free/open content, and can be accessed from the comfort of your study.

To be Sure, You will Not be Able to Access *All* (*or Even Most*) Bank Analyst Research on a Company via Public Sources

Sell-side analysts can perform analyses that are extremely costly, sophisticated, and time consuming, and they naturally want to provide first access to valued clients. Nevertheless, the portion of analyst research that finds its way to public access media can be a valuable learning tool for new alpha researchers.

Looking Up Analyst Discussions and Estimates on Finance Portals

Given the proliferation of mentions in the financial media regarding analyst research, pulling up some mention of analyst research on a company is often as easy as entering that company's stock ticker into your favorite finance portal. For instance, entering Apple's stock ticker "AAPL" into Yahoo Finance's portal turns up the headlines in Figure 23.3 in December 2014.[4]

On the left of the screenshot, it is not difficult to quickly spot headlines and links to articles that draw upon analyst research. On the right side of the page, Yahoo Finance also has very helpfully summarized analyst estimates on AAPL's earnings per share and average analyst recommendation (e.g. strong buy, sell, etc.). Clicking on the highlighted links above will generally lead to a description of a specific analyst's view on AAPL, his thought process and data for arriving at such a view, caveats, as well as price targets and recommendations.

---

[4] We chose a single portal (Yahoo Finance) as an example. You can find similar content on other mainstream finance portals such as Google Finance, Bloomberg.com, etc.

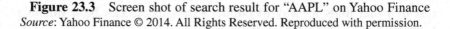

Headlines

* Pa. school district uses $291K Apple gift on iPads AP (Wed 8:52AM EST)
* Why Even Apple Is Surprised by the Enormous Demand for the iPhone 6 at TheStreet (Wed 8:45AM EST)
* I'm not loving these big phones Yahoo Finance Blogs (Wed 8:42AM EST)
* Will Apple (AAPL) Stock React Today to This Analyst Action? at TheStreet (Wed 8:35AM EST)
* Meet 5 Big Caps Whose Earnings Are Expected To Surge at Investor's Business Daily (Wed 8:02AM EST)
* TiVo is a good acquisition target for Apple, Alibaba among others: analyst at MarketWatch (Wed 7:49AM EST)
* iPhone 6S Rumors Point To A Curious Early 2015 Release at Forbes (Wed 5:08AM EST)
* Don't Confuse Morgan Stanley Decreasing Apple's Weighting By 1% With Being Negative On The Shares at Forbes (Wed 4:07AM EST)
* Apple iPod Antitrust Trial Gets Under Way at The Wall Street Journal (Wed 1:05AM EST)
* Jobs Said Apple Took Pains to Protect Record Contracts at Bloomberg (Wed 12:23AM EST)
* Mozilla wants to put Firefox on iOS at Engadget (Tue, Dec 2)
* Apple vs. Samsung in '15 at Barrons.com (Tue, Dec 2)
* Google's Chromecast Overtakes Apple TV in Video Streaming, Survey Says at The Wall Street Journal (Tue, Dec 2)
* Your first trade for Wednesday at CNBC (Tue, Dec 2)
* In emails, Jobs determined to keep iPod Apple-only AP (Tue, Dec 2)

HPQ	72.52B

» More Competitors

Key Statistics

Forward P/E (1 yr):	13.42
P/S (ttm):	3.68
Ex-Dividend Date:	06-Nov-14

» More Key Statistics

Analysts

Annual EPS Est (Sep-15):	7.74
Quarterly EPS Est (Dec-14):	2.53
Mean Recommendation*:	1.9
PEG Ratio (5 yr expected):	1.29

* (Strong Buy) 1.0 - 5.0 (Sell)

Analyst Opinion | Estimates

Business Summary

Apple Inc. designs, manufactures, and markets mobile communication and media devices, personal computers, and portable digital music players worldwide. View More

Company Profile | Industry

Figure 23.3   Screen shot of search result for "AAPL" on Yahoo Finance
Source: Yahoo Finance © 2014. All Rights Reserved. Reproduced with permission.

At the same time, you may wish to try out this process on other portals such as Google Finance, Bloomberg.com, and others, before picking the one that works best for yourself. When all else fails, try search engines directly (Google for "aapl analyst reports," for instance).

As with analyst research, it is possible to get transcripts of company's earning calls, as well as stock analyst questions and responses to those questions during the call, via finance portals. In the next example, we will use another finance portal called MorningStar, at http://www.morningstar.com (2014). This is one of the many places on the internet where you can find such information. Other examples include the SeekingAlpha website, at http://seekingalpha.com (2014), stock exchange websites (such as http://www.nasdaq.com), and the investor relations section of company websites. Some of these also contain a fair amount of discussion from non-bank market commentators on specific industries as well as stocks. The discussion on these sites may be analogous to research from stock analysts, touching on points such as firm-specific fundamentals, macroeconomics, geo-politics and market conditions. Table 23.4 provides additional examples of such market commentary/finance blog sites.

Table 23.4   Market commentary and blogs on economics and finance

Market commentary sites	Link
Bloomberg	http://www.bloomberg.com
Wall Street Journal	http://www.wsj.com
SeekingAlpha	http://www.seekingalpha.com
MorningStar	http://www.morningstar.com
TheStreet.com (only some content is free)	http://www.thestreet.com

Examples of finance blogs – by academic researchers, market analysts/commentators	Link
Econbrowser	http://econbrowser.com/
Free Exchange	http://www.economist.com/blogs/ freeexchange
Zero Hedge	http://www.zerohedge.com/
CXO Advisory	http://www.cxoadvisory.com/blog/
Freakonomics	http://freakonomics.com/
Marginal Revolution	http://marginalrevolution.com/

Note: In many places, our listing coincides with a ranking compiled by *Time* magazine. URL is http://content.time.com/time/specials/packages/completelist/0,29569,2057116,00.html.

See if you can find AAPL's Q2 2014 earnings call transcript with Analyst Q&A on the MorningStar website. If you are trying this in your browser, the important links to click on are highlighted with black rectangles (see Figure 23.4).

So Far, So Good. But Why Should You Care?

Good question. Most analyst reports (or market commentaries) focus on a single stock or industry, while you, as an alpha researcher, are looking for systematic market strategies that trade tens of thousands of stocks each day. *So what* if some analyst from Bank XYZ likes a particular company? How do we go from this to trading thousands of companies in 20 different stock exchanges across the world?

Here is why we think researchers looking for systematic market strategies can learn from reading stock analyst reports:

- **Far more important than any specific "buy" or "sell" recommendation is the analyst's thought process.** Did he decide to upgrade AAPL because of industry-specific reasons (e.g. "the market for smart-

| Membership | Home | Portfolio | Stocks | Bonds | Funds | ETFs | CEFs |

Apple Inc AAPL | ★★★

☐ Add to Portfolio   ⌀ Get E-mail Alerts   ☐ PDF Report   ? Data Question

Quote   Chart   🖽 Stock Analysis   Performance   Key Ratios   Financials   Valuation   Insiders   Ow

Q2 2014 Earnings Call Transcript

| **Presentation** | Q&A | Call Participants | ⬛ Comment 🔊 ⊞ SHARE |

Transcript Call Date 04/23/2014
Operator: Good day, everyone and welcome to the Apple Incorporated Second
Quarter Fiscal Year 2014 Earnings Release Conference Call. Today's call is being
recorded. At this time for opening remarks and introductions, I would like to turn the
call over to Nancy Paxton, Senior Director of Investor Relations. Please go ahead,
ma'am.

Nancy Paxton - IR: Thank you. Good afternoon, and thanks to everyone for joining
us today. Speaking first today are Apple's CEO, Tim Cook; and Vice President and
Corporate Controller, Luca Maestri; and they will joined by CFO, Peter Oppenheimer
for the Q&A session with Analysts.

Figure 23.4   Screen shot of Apple Inc. on MorningStar.com with highlights
Source: © 2014 Morningstar, Inc. All Rights Reserved. Reproduced with permission.

phones has been growing at triple digits"), or was it because of firm-
specific reasons (net margins have been increasing over the last four
quarters), or something more general, such as the company having a
lower price/earnings ratio compared to the rest of the industry? Regardless of the reason, one interesting question is: *Can I apply this to other
companies, too*? For instance, if the analyst says he likes AAPL because
the CEO has been buying stock in the company, should this logic be
applied only to AAPL, or to publicly-listed companies in general? This
line of reasoning has been known to yield a new strategy idea or two.

• **Analysts usually ask really good questions during earnings calls.**
They should, since they are paid a lot to do so. For a new researcher
trying to figure out how to make sense of the dense collection of
numbers that is a modern corporation's financials, these questions
can be a life saver. More information is not always better, especially if
you have 20 pages of numbers *per company*, and are trying to separate

signal from noise. How should you understand which accounting item is important? One clue is to think about which numbers or trends analysts focus on, and what they may be driving at with their questions. Are they puzzled by the extremely large and unseasonal change in inventories from one quarter to the next? Why is this important? As always, we can ask if it is something that is important beyond the company under discussion.

- **Analysts have detailed industry knowledge.** Industry-specific expertise has been cited, as Larrabee (2014) points out, as one of the most important attributes (and competitive advantages) of stock analysts. The best sell-side analysts are even able to move stock prices with their stock ratings and forecasts, and this effect is stronger among analysts with industry experience. This is relevant to researchers because there is much about methodology to be learnt from analyst work. For instance:

  - Valuation methodologies vary across industries. Constructing a discounted cash flow may be very different for the manufacturing sector compared to financials for cyclical firms, compared to non-cyclicals, etc. Analysts may focus on different valuation metrics such as price/earnings ratio for one industry, and price/book ratio for another. To the alpha researcher, it is important to understand the underlying reasons for these differences in order to generalize to the universe of tradable issues.

  - Each industry may have its own unique driver or measure of operational performance that usually features prominently in analyst reports. Dot coms used to look at "eyeballs" back in the late 1990s (perhaps they still do to some extent); airlines think about "passenger-miles"; while biotech companies may focus on drugs in the pipeline or drug trials. Understanding the key drivers of operational performance in each industry may help the alpha researcher trying to figure out inter-industry variations in her strategy performance.

- **Analyst research can provide valid trading signals.** As a bonus, analyst research can move stock prices on occasion. You may have seen headlines attributing a large price bump or fall in a specific ticker to an analyst upgrade or downgrade, increase in price targets, etc. There is an extensive body of academic research showing a link between analyst research and stock returns, which can be found on Google Scholar (2014) under "stock analyst research." A better understanding of analyst recommendations may help you make better use of this information in constructing strategies.

Things to Watch Out for in Reading Analyst Research

Whether you are reading analyst research to look for inspiration on new market strategies, or wanting to use their recommendations and targets directly in strategy construction, it may help to keep in mind some of the pros, cons, and idiosyncrasies of analyst research.

- **Positive bias.** While different banks may have different approaches, academic researchers have argued that stock analysts, as a group, could exhibit positive bias. One possible implication is that the distribution of analyst recommendations may be skewed. For example, if we think about "buy," "hold," and "sell" recommendations, there might be far more "buy" than "sell" recommendations. Academic researchers have further studied reasons for this, as argued by Michaely and Womack (1999) and Lin and McNichols (1998), which question whether banks are inclined to issue optimistic recommendations for firms that they have relationships with.
- **Herding.** Herding refers to the theory that analysts try not to be too different from one another in their public recommendations and targets. As the theory goes, part of the reason for this may be behavioral. Making public stock price predictions (or "targets," in analyst speak) is a risky endeavor with career implications. All else being equal, there may be some safety in numbers from going with the crowd. A corollary to this is that analysts who are more confident, or have established reputations, are usually willing to deviate more from consensus.
- Behavioral reasons aside, there may be sound reasons for analysts to arrive at similar conclusions – e.g. most might be working off the same sources of information. Hence, it might be interesting to understand major analyst deviations from consensus, what is unique about their analysis methods or data sources, and if this can be "systematized."

Why do Stock Analysts Talk to the Financial Media?

If you were to invest significant time and energy into detailed analysis that produces wonderful trading ideas, your first impulse may not be to pick up the telephone and tell a bunch of reporters about it. After all, many ideas are capacity limited – only so many people can trade them before the price starts to move significantly and the chance for profit disappears.

Yet we find mention of analyst research in publicly accessible media reports all the time. In fact, we may even rely on this to some extent, since it allows us to peek into the world of analyst research at almost no cost. What explains this accessibility? Possible reasons include:

- Some meetings between stock analysts and the companies they cover are open to members of the public, and often covered by the financial press. One example of this is earnings calls, which are available through publicly available transcripts. A possible reason (at least in the United States) is SEC Regulation Fair Disclosure, known as FD (www.sec.gov, 2015), which states that non-public information disclosed by issuers to investment professionals must also be made available to all market participants. This includes analysts working for huge multibillion-dollar banks as well as members of the investing public.
- Some publicity probably does not hurt a stock analyst's career. Media mentions and interviews may increase demand for an analyst's research among investor clients, and high profile recommendations that are proven right (e.g. "calling" the market bottom in 2008) may fast track an analyst's career. These are only possible if analysts go public with some of their research.

In Summary

- Analyst research may be accessible via the financial media.
- The methodologies and reasoning processes used by analysts in arriving at their recommendations may be a source of ideas for alpha researchers.
- Analyst recommendations and targets may be trading signals in their own right.
- Positive bias and analyst herding are two caveats to keep in mind.

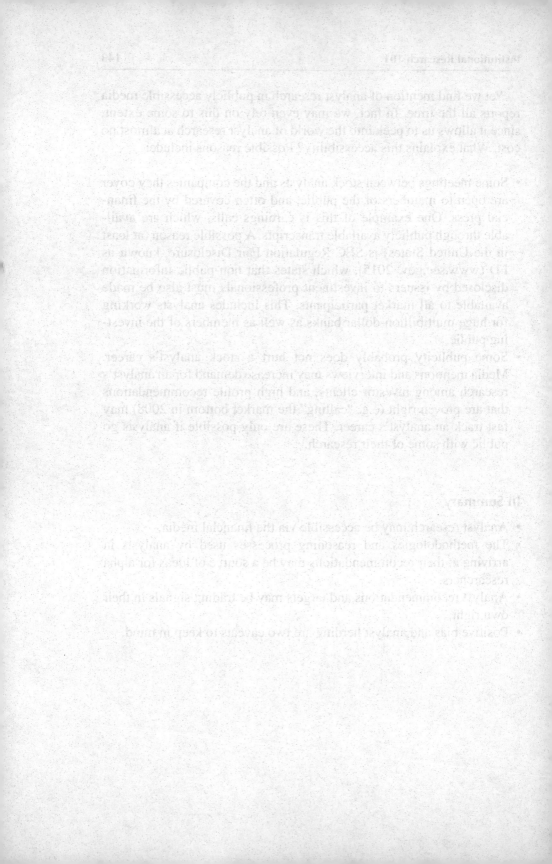

24
Introduction to Futures Trading

By Rohit Agarwal

Futures trading includes equity indices, commodities, currencies, and bonds.

An alpha is proportional to: (breadth of universe * depth of information). There are certainly a lot fewer instruments in the futures universe as compared to the equity universe – which means we need to do greater in-depth research to generate substantial alphas from them.

With futures, in contrast to equities, one property may not be comparable across the entire universe due to the diversity within the universe. This difficulty in generating alphas is compensated by the greater liquidity in these markets.

Here's a look at the most interesting, prominent, and useful information or phenomenon monitored in futures trading.

COMMITMENT OF TRADERS REPORT BY THE COMMODITY FUTURES TRADING COMMISSION

The Commitment of Traders (COT) report (Figure 24.1) is released every Friday. It can be extremely valuable in knowing what the "smart money" is betting on, and then following it. The report gives us the open interest breakdown by different market participants, such as commercial traders (big businesses/producers), non-commercial traders (large speculators), and non-reportable traders (small speculators).

```
Disaggregated Commitments of Traders-All Futures Combined Positions as of January 14, 2014
:                                    Reportable Positions                                    :
:------------------------------------------------------------------------------------------- :
: Producer/Merchant :                         :                         :                    :
:  Processor/User   :     Swap Dealers        :     Managed Money       :  Other Reportables :
:  Long  :  Short   :  Long  :  Short :Spreading:  Long  :  Short :Spreading:  Long  :  Short :Spreading :
-------------------------------------------------------------------------------------------
WHEAT-SRW - CHICAGO BOARD OF TRADE   (CONTRACTS OF 5,000 BUSHELS)
CFTC Code #001602                                         Open Interest is   422,664         :
: Positions                                                                                  :
:  69,239    79,610    94,197    15,094    13,587    95,741   152,136    44,882    38,695    32,458    32,917 :
:                                                                                            :
: Changes from:       January 7, 2014                                                        :
:  -8,010     1,077       626     1,083     1,197     6,007    -9,357     1,712    -3,748     1,405    11,273 :
:                                                                                            :
: Percent of Open Interest Represented by Each Category of Trader                            :
:   16.4       18.8      22.3       3.6       3.2      22.7      36.0      10.6       9.2       7.7       7.8 :
:                                                                                            :
: Number of Traders in Each Category                          Total Traders:   384           :
:     72         72        15         8        16        40        89        56        62        64        62 :
```

Figure 24.1   COT report of wheat for the week ending January 2014
Source: U.S. Commodity Futures Trading Association (Jan, 2014)

More about this report can be learned here:
http://www.cftc.gov/marketreports/commitmentsoftraders/index
.htm

SEASONALITY IN MARKETS

Seasonality is the tendency of markets to move in a given direction at certain times of the year. It is a prominent behavior observed in agri-commodity markets due to weather cycles. But it is not restricted to just agri-commodities as it can be in play due to cyclical demand, consumption, inventory, or supply patterns as well.

Figure 24.2 shows the seasonality in natural gas reserves or inventory. As winter approaches, the demand for natural gas increases as inventory reduces due to its use in the heating of homes.

Past performance may not guarantee future results.

RISK ON AND RISK OFF

There are times when market sentiment is positive, and investors are optimistic and willing to take more risk in order to get better returns. Such an environment is called a "risk-on" market because risk taking is on. On the other hand, there are times when investors are pessimistic and try to cut risk by selling their positions in risky assets and moving

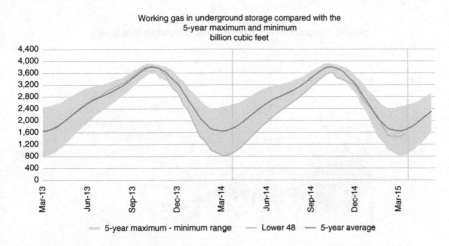

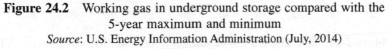

Figure 24.2 Working gas in underground storage compared with the 5-year maximum and minimum
Source: U.S. Energy Information Administration (July, 2014)

money to cash positions or low-risk safe havens, like US Treasury bonds. These are called "risk-off" times (Figure 24.3).

This investor behavior – to flock toward assets perceived as risky during risk-on times, and assets perceived as risk-free during risk-off times – increases the correlation between different asset classes.

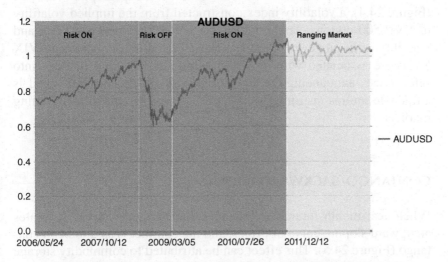

Figure 24.3 Risk-on/risk-off regimes on the AUD/USD price curve

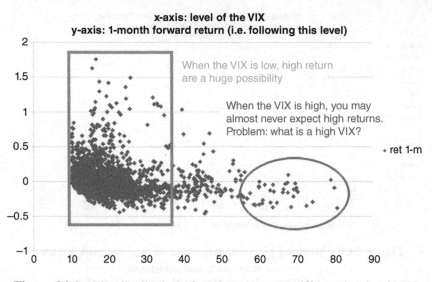

Figure 24.4   The distribution of market returns at different levels of VIX

The steps to successfully construct risk-on/risk-off strategies include identifying whether the market is in a risk-on or risk-off regime on a daily/weekly/monthly/quarterly basis, and then categorizing different assets as risk-on assets or risk-off assets, and taking positions in them.

One such popular indicator of market risk perception is VIX (Figure 24.4), a volatility index constructed from the implied volatility of S&P 500 options. Traditionally, the correlation between price and volatility is negative for equities. Therefore, high or increasing VIX levels are associated with money moving out of equity markets into safer assets, announcing the arrival of a risk-off regime. VIX itself is a tradable futures instrument and used by many to benefit from falling markets.

CONTANGO/BACKWARDATION

When near-month futures are cheaper than farther expiries, it creates an upward sloping curve of prices, and the contract is said to be in contango (Figure 24.5). This effect can be attributed to commodity storage cost or cost of carry.

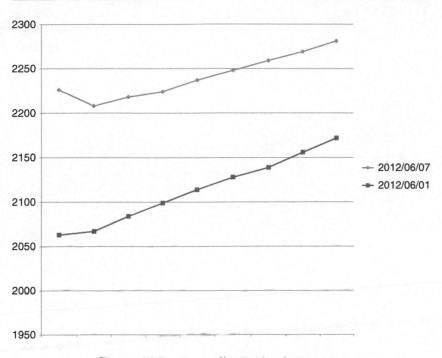

Figure 24.5 Cocoa distribution in contango

However, in some cases it is possible that near-month futures are more expensive than far-month futures, which creates a downward sloping curve and the contract is said to be in backwardation.

Some traders make money by selling contracts in contango and buying contracts in backwardation.

While these are some of the widely-researched topics in futures trading, the scope is vast and extends into many more territories.

25
Alpha on Currency Forwards and Futures
By Richard Williams

Finding alpha within the currencies and futures markets is an area of great practical interest. It also presents many challenges, as has already been noted in this book. In this chapter we will discuss some of the techniques and habits of thought that have been useful in attacking this problem over the last few years.

KEY MARKET FEATURES

Futures, in particular, are designed to give the trader exposure to price changes in the underlying market without necessarily having to fund owning the equivalent position in the underlying asset. Within the context of alpha research, short dated forwards on currencies provide the same sort of framework for accessing relative currency value. This means that futures and forwards are extremely convenient instruments for both hedgers and speculators, and give rise to probably the most significant feature we want to consider.

UNDERLYING FACTOR EXPOSURE

Since both futures and forwards give exposure equivalent to the underlying, it follows that the factors affecting the underlying assets are the ones that drive the price of the future/forward. This simple observation has important implications: there are distinct groups of market traders who are focused on particular groups of futures and currencies; these are the hedgers looking to control their risks to particular factors. Good examples are provided by the commodity futures, where producers and consumers of physical commodities hedge their risk on specific commodities. For example, the farmers and food producing corporations that use the agricultural markets extensively to control their risks have little in common with the airlines who make extensive use of energy futures to hedge their future fuel costs. Each group of traders can have their own characteristic risk limits, tolerances, and trading behaviors, which in turn can give rise to qualitatively different market behavior.

In recognition of these differences between market users, it is traditional within many organizations to have specialists managing the trading of different classes of futures and currencies, with the classes based on grouping sets of similar, underlying assets. This further reinforces the differences between "sectors," as different traders, desks, and business lines are all managing different futures and forwards.

CONSEQUENCES OF INSTRUMENT GROUPING

The instrument groups discussed above give us both opportunities and challenges in seeking alpha. One of the most obvious challenges is that, as we consider smaller groups of more closely-connected instruments, we have fewer things we can actually trade. Therefore, we require stronger structure per instrument than we do to achieve the same aggregate results with a larger instrument set. As the quality of the per-instrument alpha increases, it becomes more obvious to other market participants and its expected lifetime is reduced. Conversely, as we identify sets of similar instruments, we have greater expectations that any particular alpha should be present across the whole set. The test of deleting each instrument in turn, and retesting the identified relationship, becomes more meaningful. These instrument groups often become the basic units on which we test our alpha candidates.

BASIC CHECKLIST FOR ALPHA TESTING

We start from the core alpha idea; the first step is to identify the sectors where we expect it to appear, and the timescales on which we expect it to manifest. As an example, let us consider the US energy market and an alpha based on the forecast of extreme weather in a major offshore US oil and gas field. Before we even consider the data, we can identify the instruments we expect to be relevant – oil, gas, and their products – and the timescale we expect the data to have an impact on, in this case including how long a typical storm lasts and how long it takes to stop and restart production (there will be a range of views on both of these horizons, but we can still use the implied causal relationship between the extreme weather and the commodity supply to narrow the range of candidates). We can now test the claim by getting the historic weather forecasts and price changes for the major energy contracts, and test for association between the two datasets, using a partial in-sample historic dataset.

The next step is to fit a simple, statistical model and test robustness, as well as varying parameters in the fit. One good robustness test is to include a similar asset where we expect the effect to be less strong. In the case of our example above, Brent crude oil would be a reasonable choice. Crude oil is a global market, so we would expect some spillover from a US supply disruption. However, oil delivered in Europe is not a perfect substitute for the US supply, so we would expect a diluted impact. Again, we can test this with in-sample data.

Having investigated where we would expect the alpha to work, we can now test the converse: Where do we expect there to be no relationship? In the case of our example, it is quite closely targeted to one sector so we would expect to detect no relationship if we retested in different sectors such as industrial metals or bond futures. This step is surprisingly good at finding incorrectly coded or specified statistical tests.

Depending on the results of the above, we could now be in a position to test our idea on our own out-of-sample dataset. With such a small set of instruments, the out-of-sample test becomes a crucial part of the process, helping to avoid unintentional overfitting.

SUMMARY

The grouping of instruments into sectors based on the underlying asset is important, with both common and distinct groups of market actors across and within these sectors providing a mechanical connection between these instruments. If you take a moment to consider how the factor exposure of each sector should respond to the idea you are exploring, you will find a useful place to start testing your ideas.

PART IV
New Horizon – WebSim™

26
Introduction to WebSim™

By Jeffrey Scott

Historically, we have created alphas using a sophisticated and proprietary simulation platform. This simulation environment allows researchers to backtest their alphas using multiple datasets including fundamental and price/volume data.

Datasets can include company performance metrics like quarterly earnings, cash flow, and return on assets and liabilities; price/volume data may include opening and closing prices, high and low prices in a specified interval, volume-weighted average price, and daily volume.

Initially, while this model was effective, it had some limitations including the following:

- Researchers needed access to the WorldQuant network to access the simulation platform.
- Since the system was available only across the corporate network, researchers were required to be full-time employees and physically located in a WorldQuant office.
- Most researchers needed to have programming expertise and work with C++.

Over the years, we developed an extensive library of alphas to be used in trading strategies. Our goal, however, was to substantially increase the number and types of alphas available to our portfolio managers. The limitations above imposed restrictions on the speed and level of growth we could achieve.

To overcome these obstacles, we began to consider options. *What if...*

...the simulation platform was placed in the cloud as a web-enabled application?
...we engaged part-time research consultants?
...we removed the obstacle of programming languages and appealed to a broader audience?
...we could tap into one of the most knowledgeable and motivated resource pools available: university students?

And so began the genesis of WebSim™...

WebSim™ is a proprietary, web-based simulation platform. Used as a foundation in the core functionality available in our internal simulation engine, WebSim™ was designed as a completely web-enabled application. As a web-based tool, it is accessible 24/7 via any browser.

Its remote availability means that users can be located in various geographic locations, so long as an internet connection is available. Even current university students can create alphas in their spare time without any specific time or location requirements.

Using WebSim™, users create alphas based on their ideas for trading strategies. These ideas are then submitted via the WebSim™ website and backtested against actual historical data to determine how effective they would have been if applied to past market periods.

To avoid having to deal with structured programming languages, a simple command line was implemented to enter alpha expressions as shown in Figure 26.1.

Using this command line, users can enter simple or complex formulas using various data elements, which may include fundamental or technical data. For those with a deeper programming background, Python scripting and libraries are available as an alternative option to creating alphas as illustrated in Figure 26.2.

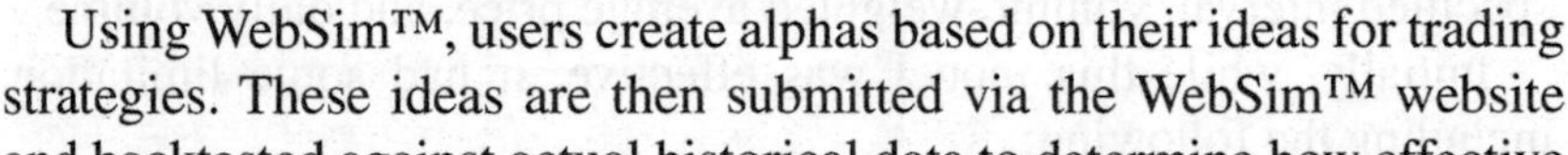

```
volume/adv20
```

Submit   Random

Figure 26.1 Command line for user to enter alpha expressions

Alpha Examples in Python

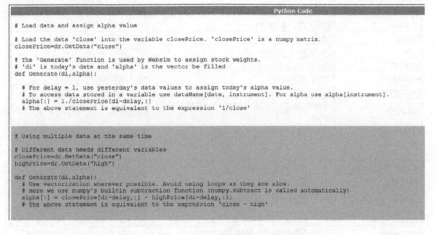

```
                                          Python Code

# Load data and assign alpha value

# Load the data 'close' into the variable closePrice. 'closePrice' is a numpy matrix.
closePrice=dr.GetData("close")

# The 'Generate' function is used by Websim to assign stock weights.
# 'di' is today's date and 'alpha' is the vector be filled
def Generate(di,alpha):

    # For delay = 1, use yesterday's data values to assign today's alpha value.
    # To access data stored in a variable use dataName[date, instrument]. For alpha use alpha[instrument].
    alpha[:] = 1./closePrice[di-delay,:]
    # The above statement is equivalent to the expression '1/close'


# Using multiple data at the same time

# Different data needs different variables
closePrice=dr.GetData("close")
highPrice=dr.GetData("high")

def Generate(di,alpha):
    # Use vectorization wherever possible. Avoid using loops as they are slow.
    # Here we use numpy's builtin subtraction function (numpy.subtract is called automatically)
    alpha[:] = closePrice[di-delay,:] - highPrice[di-delay,:];
    # The above statement is equivalent to the expression 'close - high'
```

Figure 26.2 Alpha examples in Python

Alphas can be created using fundamental data, price/volume data, or a combination of the two. Various settings are available so a user can run an alpha on diverse "universe settings," such as the number of equities to use, or the desired timeframe for backtesting.

Figure 26.3 is a sample list of data fields that are available for Web-Sim expressions. This list is not all-inclusive and is provided simply to reflect the types of available data.

In addition to the data fields, the user can create expressions using a variety of mathematical operators, a sampling of which is provided in Figure 26.4. Again this is not an all-inclusive list, and is provided for sample purposes only.

WebSim™ will take the results of the alpha simulation and instantaneously display them for the user to review. Factors such as overall PnL, Sharpe Ratio, and Daily Turnover are immediately visible to determine the effectiveness of the alpha as can be seen in Figure 26.5. Users can then fine-tune their idea with variations on the alpha parameters in an effort to improve its rating.

WebSim™ users have access to a dashboard highlighting alphas they have created, along with rating categories, so they can constantly measure their own work. High-quality alphas are processed using Out-Sample testing for further analysis.

Data Name	Description	Python Usage
open	Daily open price	dr.GetData("open")
close	Daily close price	dr.GetData("close")
high	Daily high price	dr.GetData("high")
low	Daily low price	dr.GetData("low")
vwap	Daily volume weighted price	dr.GetData("vwap")
volume	Daily volume	dr.GetData("volume")
returns	Daily returns	dr.GetData("returns")
adv20	Average daily volume in past 20 days	dr.GetData("adv20")
sharesout	Daily outstanding shares	dr.GetData("sharesout")

Data Name	Description	Python Usage
sales	Quarterly Sales	dr.GetData("sales")
sales_growth	Growth in Quarterly Sales	dr.GetData ("sales_growth")
sales_ps	Quarterly Sales Per share	dr.GetData("sales_ps")
income	Quarterly Net Income	dr.GetData("income")
eps	Earnings Per Share	dr.GetData("eps")
cashflow	Quarterly Cashflow	dr.GetData("cashflow")
cashflow_op	Quarterly Cashflow From Operating Activities	dr.GetData ("cashflow_op")
cashflow_fin	Quarterly Cashflow From Financial Activities	dr.GetData ("cashflow_fin")
cashflow_invst	Quarterly Cashflow From Investments	dr.GetData ("cashflow_invst")
cashflow_dividends	Quarterly Cashflow From Dividends	dr.GetData ("cashflow_dividends")
assets_curr	Current Assets	dr.GetData ("assets_curr")
assets	Total Assets	dr.GetData("assets")
equity	Common Equity	dr.GetData("equity")
debt_lt	Long Term Debt	dr.GetData("debt_lt")
debt_st	Short Term Debt	dr.GetData("debt_st")
debt	Total Debt	dr.GetData("debt")
liabilities_curr	Current Liabilities	dr.GetData ("liabilities_curr")
liabilities	Total Liabilities	dr.GetData("liabilities")
EBITDA	Earnings Before Interest, Tax, Depreciation and Amortization	dr.GetData("EBITDA")
capex	Capital Expenditure	dr.GetData("capex")
operating_income	Operating Income	dr.GetData ("operating_income")
operating_expense	Operating Expenses	dr.GetData ("operating_expense")
cogs	Cost of Goods Sold	dr.GetData("cogs")
bookvalue_ps	Bookvalue Per Share	dr.GetData ("bookvalue_ps")

Figure 26.3 Sample list of data fields for WebSim™ expressions

Operator	Description	ReturnType
+, -, *, /, ^	Add, Subtract, Multiply, Divide, Power	Vector
<, <=, >, >=, ==, !=	Logic comparison operators	Vector
||, &&, !	Logical OR, AND, Negation	Vector
cond ? expr1 : expr2	If cond is true, expr1; else expr2. For example, close < open ? close : open	Vector
Rank(x)	Rank the values of x among all instruments, and the return values are float numbers equally distributed between 0.0 and 1.0. For example, given 6 stocks with close price [20.2, 15.6, 10.0, 5.7, 50.2, 18.4], rank(close) returns [0.8, 0.4, 0.2, 0.0, 1.0, 0.6].	Vector
Min(x, y)	Parallel minimum of vectors x and y (similar to the pmin function in R). This takes 2 vectors as arguments and returns a single vector giving the 'parallel' minima of the vectors. The first element of the result is the minimum of the first elements of all the arguments, the second element of the result is the minimum of the second elements of all the arguments and so on.	Vector
Max(x, y)	Parallel maximum of vectors x and y (similar to the pmax function in R). This takes 2 vectors as arguments and returns a single vector giving the 'parallel' maxima of the vectors. The first element of the result is the maximum of the first elements of both the arguments, the second element of the result is the maximum of the second elements of both the arguments and so on.	Vector
StdDev(x, n)	Standard deviation of the values in vector x for the past n days. Note that n must be less than 256	Scalar
Correlation(x, y, n)	Correlation of the values in vectors x and y for the past n days. Note that n must be less than 256	Scalar

Figure 26.4 Partial list of mathematical operators for creating alpha expressions *(Continues)*

Tail(x, lower, upper, newval)	Set the values of x to newval if they are between lower and upper	Vector
Ts_Min(x, n)	Minimum value of x over the last n days. Note that this is different than Min	Vector
Ts_Max(x, n)	Maximum value of x over the last n days. Note that this is different than Max	Vector
Sum_i(expr, var, start, stop, step)	Loop over var (from start to stop with step) and calculate expr at every iteration (presumably expr would contain var), then sum over all the values. For example: `Sum_i(Delay(close, i)*i, i, 2, 4, 1)` would be equivalent to `Delay(close, 2)*2 + Delay(close, 3)*3 + Delay(close, 4)*4`	Scalar
Call_i(expr, var, subexpr)	Substitute subexpr for var in expr, and then evaluate expr. For example, `Call_i(x + 4, x, 2 + 3)` would be equivalent to (2 + 3) + 4	Vector
Sign(x)	Returns 1 if x > 0, -1 if x < 0, 0 if x == 0	Vector
SignedPower (x, e)	`Sign(x) * (Abs(x)^e)`	Vector
Pasteurize(x)	Pasteurize the signals. Set to NaN if it is INF or if the underlying instrument is not in the universe	Vector
Log(x)	Natural logarithm	Vector
Ts_Rank(x, n)	Rank the values of x of the same instrument over the past n days, then return the rank of the current value. The rank value is between 0.0 ~ 1.0, as illustrated in the explanation of Rank(x).	Vector
Ts_Skewness (x, n)	Compute the skewness of x on the last n days	Scalar
Ts_Kurtosis(x, n)	Compute the kurtosis of x on the last n days.	Scalar
Ts_Moment(x, k, n)	Compute the kth central moment of x on the last n days	Scalar
IndNeutralize (x, y)	Neutralize Alpha x against groupings specified by y. For example, `IndNeutralize(x, industry)` and `IndNeutralize(x, subindustry)` to neutralize against industries and subindustries respectively. To neutralize against market, use `IndNeutralize(x, 1)`	Vector

Figure 26.4 (*Continued*)

Year	Book Size	Long Count	Short Count	Pnl	Sharpe	Fitness	Returns	Drawdown	Turnover	Margin
2009	20.0M	1311	1212	1.86M	3.55	2.13	19.67%	1.18%	54.76%	7.18 bpm
2010	20.0M	1395	1302	1.35M	3.11	1.54	13.40%	1.38%	54.71%	4.90 bpm
2011	20.0M	1385	1341	1.15M	1.94	0.88	11.38%	2.65%	55.41%	4.11 bpm
2012	20.0M	1407	1332	948K	2.44	1.00	9.48%	1.14%	56.19%	3.37 bpm
2013	20.0M	1426	1293	706K	1.89	0.67	7.01%	1.18%	55.61%	2.52 bpm
2009-2013	20.0M	1386	1297	6.02M	2.55	1.19	12.10%	2.65%	55.34%	4.37 bpm

Figure 26.5 WebSim™ simulation summary

27
Alphas and WebSim™ Fundamentals

By the WebSim™ Team

With the development of information technology, information processing, automatic trading, etc., the market is always close to 100% efficiency but is never at 100%. We seek to arbitrage profit from this inefficiency.

It is difficult to predict one stock's future return. One stock error due to noisy data will not hurt the whole performance. The process of betting many stocks every day is called statistical arbitrage, which is what WebSim™ does.

Statistical arbitrages are also called alphas. *A good statistical arbitrage model usually involves a large number of securities and may have short holding periods, with positive returns expected in the long run.*

ALPHAS AND WEBSIM™

An alpha is a mathematical, predictive model of the performance of financial instruments (e.g. stocks, futures contracts, etc.) that can be simulated historically using WebSim™. This model is comprised of data (e.g. close price, open price, volume, etc.) and mathematical expressions (+/−, StdDev(x, n), regression, etc.).

WebSim™ is a web-based simulator of global financial markets that was created to explore alpha research. It will accept an alpha expression/Python code as input and will plot its PnL as its output. The input expression is evaluated for each financial instrument, every day (history dates), and a portfolio is constructed accordingly. WebSim™

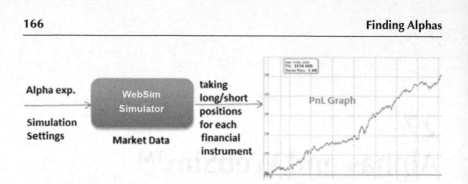

Figure 27.1 The generation of a PnL graph in WebSim™ simulator

invests in each financial instrument to the value of the expression. It either takes a long or short position, based on which a PnL graph is plotted, as can be seen in Figure 27.1.

Since the PnL is generated for historical data, it is called the In-Sample PnL. After the alpha is submitted, it has to pass some criteria set by WebSim™. If it passes the criteria, it will be evaluated against real-time data for a period known as Out-Sample (OS) period. The PnL generated in this case, as seen in Figure 27.2, is called OutSample PnL

For assembling alphas into a portfolio, different weights are placed on different alphas. The weights are then scaled to book size when calculating PnL. These weights are not constants; they change over time based on the current information and the history of the changes of some variables (such as prices, volumes, etc.).

ALPHA SOURCES

Alpha ideas can be found online via research papers, finance journals, and technical indicators.

Technical indicators are used for analyzing short-term price movements. They are derived from generic price activity in a stock/asset. They predict the future price levels or the general price direction of a security by looking at the past patterns. Examples of common technical indicators are Relative Strength Index, Money Flow Index, MACD, Bollinger Bands, etc. You can find their explanation, formulae, and corresponding interpretation in websites like Stock Charts, Incredible Charts, etc.

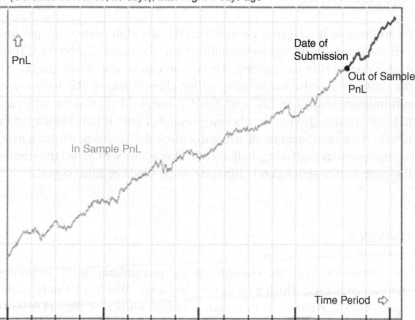

Figure 27.2 Out-Sample PnL generated in WebSim™

SSRN is a good place to start if you are looking for alpha ideas. And so are websites like Seeking Alpha and Wilmott.

Blogs are a good source of alpha research too, e.g. Epchan, AuTraSy, etc.

Concepts to explore:

- Price movement and technical indicator.
- Volatility measures – historical volatility, implied volatility, volatility index, intraday volatility, etc.
- Volume's interaction with price – volume is positively correlated with absolute price changes, etc.
- Short-term and long-term trends – http://www.investopedia.com/articles/technical/03/060303.asp.

The user should note that any reference to third-party sites above is for the user's convenience only. Users should read and abide by the terms of use of these sites.

NEUTRALIZATION

Neutralization is an operation in which the raw alpha values are put into various groups, followed by normalization (the mean is subtracted from each value) within each group. The group can be the entire market. Or the groups could be made using other classifications like industry or sub-industry (based on SIC and NAICS codes). This is done so as not to bet in the direction of the chosen group, but only relative stock future return. As a consequence of neutralization, the entire portfolio carries neutral position (half long, half short). Doing this will guard the portfolio from market shocks and eliminate some kinds of false signals.

UNIVERSE

The simulation universe consists of the instruments to be evaluated and the dates over which evaluations are done. WebSim™ only trades liquid stocks. WebSim™ provides standard universes like TOP3000, TOP2000, TOP1000, etc.

The TOP-N universes are comprised of N stocks of the region with the highest average dollar volume over the past three months. For example, in the top liquid universes, TOP3000 is a set of 3,000 stocks with highest liquidity in a three-month period; TOP2000 is a set of 2,000 stocks with highest liquidity in a three-month period; and so on. TOP2000 is a subset of TOP3000 stocks.

28
Understanding How WebSim™ Works

By the WebSim™ Team

Imagine market data being a matrix, each row representing one date and each column representing one stock. For example, the matrix for close price data of stocks in Universe TOP3000 would look like Table 28.1.

And the matrix for volume data of the above stocks would look like Table 28.2.

If you enter an alpha expression in the WebSim™ homepage and set the simulation period for five years, WebSim™ will evaluate the input alpha expression against the matrix of market data for each date of the last five years, from the oldest date to today.

On each iteration/day, the expression will have access to all the data up to today and the matrix will grow by one line every day, until it reaches the recent date.

The role of the expression is to transform the input matrix to an output vector of weights.

The alpha output vector having alpha weights as values corresponding to each instrument in the Universe would look something like Table 28.3.

For each day, the expression is evaluated and the values in the alpha output vector represent how many instruments (stock or contact) you want to buy or sell. The value of the vector is not the number of shares you want to buy, but the weight you want to give to a position, relative to other stocks. A positive number would signify a buy, a negative number would signify a sell, and a NaN value would mean no alpha weight is allocated to that instrument (i.e. no fund is allocated). When the alpha position is NaN,

Table 28.1 Matrix for close price data of stocks in Universe TOP3000

Instruments Dates	MSFT	HOG	AAPL	GOOG	PG	...
20100104	30.95	25.46	214.01	626.75	61.12	...
20100105	30.96	25.65	214.38	623.99	61.14	...
20100106	30.77	25.59	210.97	608.26	60.85	...
20100107	30.452	25.8	210.58	594.1	60.52	...
20100108	30.66	25.53	211.98	602.02	60.44	...
...	...	...	...	...	...	...

no PnL will be generated for it. Based on those daily positions, PnL is then calculated and displayed to the user. By default, WebSim™ will normalize your weights and create a portfolio of $20 million worth of equity.

SIMULATION SETTINGS PANEL

An alpha has features like asset class, delay, etc., which can be specified for a simulation in the simulation settings panel before it commences. The settings panel (gear icon) can be found at the top right-hand corner of the WebSim™ Home page. The different setting parameters are given in Figure 28.1.

Asset Class: WebSim™ currently supports two classes of instruments: Equity (stocks) and Futures. Other asset classes like currencies, exchange-traded funds, etc. will be added soon.

Region and Universe: The only region available currently is the US market. WebSim™ will expand to other regions like Europe and Asia. Universe is a set of trading instruments prepared by WebSim™. For example, "US: TOP3000" represents the top 3,000 most liquid stocks in the US market, while "US: EQ Index Futures" represents the set of futures for US equity indices.

Delay: Delay refers to the availability of data relative to decision time. Delay 1 (which is set by default) means that the alpha will use yesterday's data (prices, returns, etc.). Delay 0 would mean that alpha will use today's data. Though it would be great to know the returns for today ahead of time, we must include the delay in order to make the simulation realistic.

Table 28.2 The matrix for volume data of stocks in Universe TOP3000

Instruments Dates	MSFT	HOG	AAPL	GOOG	PG
20100101	3.84142e+07	2.90391e+06	1.76332e+07	1.95796e+06	9.19087e+06
20100102	4.97589e+07	2.80537e+06	2.14966e+07	3.00786e+06	8.65051e+06
20100103	5.81823e+07	3.2833e+06	1.97199e+07	3.98063e+06	9.90891e+06
20100104	5.05643e+07	2.52213e+06	1.70403e+07	6.41802e+06	8.97275e+06
20100105	5.12013e+07	3.52372e+06	1.59956e+07	4.72474e+06	8.46696e+06
⋮	⋮	⋮	⋮	⋮	⋮

Table 28.3 Alpha weights as values corresponding to each instrument in the Universe TOP3000

Instruments	MSFT	HOG	AAPL	GOOG	PG	...
Alpha weights	0.2423	0.5675	−0.4745	0.4734	−0.5684	...

Decay: This performs a linear decay function over the past n days by combining today's value with previous days' decayed value. It performs the following function:

$$\text{Decay\_linear}(x, n) = (x[\text{date}] * n + x[\text{date} - 1] * (n - 1) + \ldots \\ + x[\text{date} - n - 1]) / (n + (n - 1) + \ldots + 1)$$

Neutralization: Neutralization is an operation used to make our strategy market/industry/sub-industry neutral. When Neutralization = "market," it does the following operation:

$$\text{alpha} = \text{alpha} - \text{mean}(\text{alpha})$$

Basically, it makes the mean of the alpha vector zero, thus no "net" position is taken with respect to the market. In other words, the long positions cancel out the short positions completely, making our strategy market neutral.

When Neutralization = "industry" or "sub-industry," all the instruments in the alpha vector are grouped into smaller buckets corresponding

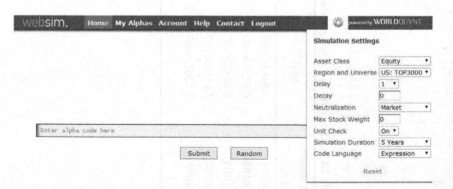

Figure 28.1 Setting parameters for WebSim™ simulation

to industry or sub-industry, and Neutralization is applied separately to each of the buckets.

Max Instrument Weight: It is the maximum weight for each instrument (stock or contract) in the overall portfolio. When it is set 0, there is no restriction.

Unit Check: This makes sure the units (dollars, etc.) match in the expression. Suppose the alpha is a nonsensical mathematical expression like: adv20 + close, which is essentially volume + price. This alpha cannot be considered as a good one. The alpha can be checked internally in WebSim™ by turning on the Unit Check setting, which checks if the corresponding units match.

Simulation Duration: This signifies the amount of history data that needs backtesting. You can set this to two or five years for Equity, and five to ten years for Futures.

Code Language: To enter a one-line alpha expression, select "Expression." To enter an alpha using Python script, select "Python."

RUN YOUR FIRST ALPHA

To run your first simulation, open the WebSim™ Home page. Click on the gear icon at the top right-hand side corner. This will open the settings panel. Here select "5 years" for Simulation duration, "US: TOP3000" for Region and Universe, "None" for Neutralization, and save your settings. In the alpha expression text box, enter "1" for now (this will ensure that all the values of the resulting vector will assign the same weight for all stocks). The Simulation Result page will show a graph for Cumulative Profit. This graph can be zoomed in to plot an area for shorter time periods (one month, three months, one year, etc.).

The Cumulative Profits graph and Sharp Ratio graph for your alpha are shown in Figures 28.2 and 28.3. The simulation results (Returns, Sharpe, Drawdown, etc.) for each year along with cumulative results are given in Figure 28.4.

The Cumulative Profit graph consists of two graphs, one for PnL vs. Time, and the other for Sharpe Ratio vs. Time. Right below the graph is a table that shows the simulation result for each year and cumulative

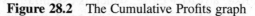

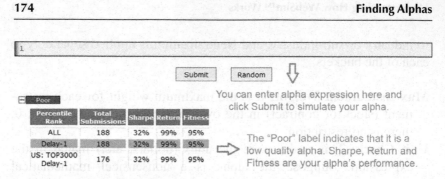

Figure 28.2   The Cumulative Profits graph

Figure 28.3   Sharpe Ratio graph

Year	Booksize	Pnl	Ann. return	Sharpe ratio	Max drawdown	% profitable days	Daily turnover	Profit per $ traded
2008	2.0E6	-5.04E6	-65.33%	-0.66	138.47%	49.74%	0.50%	-26.09 ¢
2009	2.0E7	9.87E6	98.30%	1.39	74.18%	55.38%	0.53%	37.36 ¢
2010	2.0E7	5.56E6	55.17%	1.22	37.28%	57.54%	0.32%	34.59 ¢
2011	2.0E7	-878.02E3	-8.78%	-0.15	66.91%	54.00%	0.33%	-5.36 ¢
2012	2.0E7	3.33E6	33.43%	1.05	29.27%	51.00%	0.31%	21.91 ¢
2013	2.0E7	1.99E6	108.00%	4.53	7.23%	71.74%	0.30%	73.13 ¢
2008 - 2013	2.0E7	14.83E6	29.87%	0.48	138.47%	54.39%	0.39%	15.42 ¢

Figure 28.4 The simulation results (Returns, Sharpe, Drawdown, etc.) for each year along with cumulative results

result for the entire simulation duration. A good alpha would have consistently increasing PnL and high Annual Return, Sharpe Ratio, % Profitable Days, and Profit per Dollar Traded. It should have low Drawdown and Turnover. And, more importantly, it shouldn't have high fluctuations in the cumulative profit graph. If the standard deviation is low, there would be lesser fluctuations in the graph. If the graph shows high fluctuations/volatility, despite the returns being high, the alpha will not be deemed good enough. An alpha is considered to be good if:

- Its Sharpe should be greater than 3.95 for delay 0 alphas, and above 2.5 for delay 1 alphas.
- Its Turnover is low (50% or lower).
- Its Percentage Drawdown should be less than 10%.

As you can see from the graph above (which has been zoomed in to show the PnL between January and October 2011), for alpha expression 1, it is an average simulation result. The fluctuations are high when you see the graph as a whole. From the table, you can see that for the year 2011, the PnL dips, the Sharpe Ratio falls below threshold, the Drawdown is enormous and the Profit per $ Traded is negative. Hence, this is an average simulation result as it lacks consistency.

ANOTHER SAMPLE ALPHA

Let's try another example using the available market data fields here. Let's use close (daily close price) and sharesout (daily outstanding shares) as the alpha expression. Now open your WebSim™ Home page again, and hover over the Settings gear button, select "5 years" for Simulation duration, "US:TOP3000" for Region and Universe, "none" for Neutralization, and save your settings. In the alpha expression text box, type in "sharesout*close" and submit the expression. Outstanding shares when multiplied by close price of a stock would signify the market cap for that stock. Since this expression is calculated for every day and every stock, the PnL will look similar to that of a commercial benchmark. Take Russell 3000, for example, as a benchmark, which you can find on Yahoo Finance. Make sure you start a new browser tab

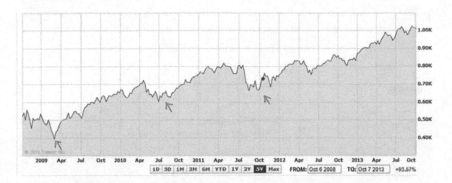

Figure 28.5   Sample of Russell 3000 Index's graph

(outside WebSim™) to search for the index and the result should look like Figure 28.5.

As you can notice from the sample Russell 3000 Index's graph above, you will see three dips in the market, one around April 2009, the second on July 2010, and the third on October 2011. Now, if you compare it with your WebSim™ simulation result (shown in Figure 28.6), you will find that both graphs have dips around the same months.

Let's take a closer look at the simulation result table as shown in Figure 28.6. As you can see, the total amount of capital invested every year (aka Book size) is $20 million. In year 2009, the PnL generated was $6.75 million and the annual return expressed in percentage is 67.01%, which is the maximum PnL generated in all 5 years. If you look at the Sharpe Ratio's column, there is a significant dip in 2010 and 2011 (as shown in the graph). The Maximum Drawdown in 2011 corresponds to the dip shown in the graph.

You could try looking through journals, websites, and blogs for alpha expressions, or use the example expressions given in this documentation as a starting point.

Figure 28.6   WebSim™ simulation result of Russell 3000 Index's graph

29
API Reference
By the WebSim™ Team

This chapter can be used as a handy reference guide to all operators and data fields that can be used for building alphas.

AVAILABLE MARKET DATA

The available market data fields given in Table 29.1 can be used in your alpha expression.

Open, high, low, close, volume, vwap, and sharesout represent data that has been carefully adjusted for corporate actions (such as dividend, split, reverse split, etc.) and ready to be used for alpha computation. As a comparison, raw price or volume is actually not ready for direct usage in alpha code; without this distinction, alpha will be unstable.

This can be explained in an example: suppose GOOG (Google) will split 2:1 on April 2 and its current price is at $1,200.

On April 3, it would likely be around $600. Without adjusting, raw price alone will distort the price action.

Adjusted data must be updated every day. For efficiency, WebSim™ calculates only for a fixed look-back period. This is defined as "Look-back days."

Company fundamental data is listed in Table 29.2 and is based on quarterly/annual statements that public companies file with their regulators.

Table 29.1   Price volume data for equity

Data name	Description	Python usage
Open	Daily open price	dr.GetData("open")
Close	Daily close price	dr.GetData("close")
High	Daily high price	dr.GetData("high")
Low	Daily low price	dr.GetData("low")
Vwap	Daily volume weighted price	dr.GetData("vwap")
Volume	Daily volume	dr.GetData("volume")
Returns	Daily returns	dr.GetData("returns")
adv20	Average daily volume in past 20 days	dr.GetData("adv20")
sharesout	Daily outstanding shares	dr.GetData("sharesout")

Table 29.2   Company fundamental data for equity

Data name	Description	Python usage
Sales	Quarterly Sales	dr.GetData("sales")
sales_growth	Growth in Quarterly Sales	dr.GetData("sales_growth")
sales_ps	Quarterly Sales Per share	dr.GetData("sales_ps")
Income	Quarterly Net Income	dr.GetData("income")
Eps	Earnings Per Share	dr.GetData("eps")
cashflow	Quarterly Cashflow	dr.GetData("cashflow")
cashflow_sales	Quarterly Cashflow From Sales	dr.GetData("cashflow_sales")
cashflow_op	Quarterly Cashflow From Operating Activities	dr.GetData("cashflow_op")
cashflow_fin	Quarterly Cashflow From Financial Activities	dr.GetData("cashflow_fin")
cashflow_invst	Quarterly Cashflow From Investments	dr.GetData("cashflow_invst")
cashflow_dividends	Quarterly Cashflow From Dividends	dr.GetData("cashflow_dividends")
assets_curr	Current Assets	dr.GetData("assets_curr")
Assets	Total Assets	dr.GetData("assets")
Equity	Common Equity	dr.GetData("equity")
debt_lt	Long Term Debt	dr.GetData("debt_lt")
debt_st	Short Term Debt	dr.GetData("debt_st")
Debt	Total Debt	dr.GetData("debt")

Data name	Description	Python usage
liabilities_curr	Current Liabilities	dr.GetData("liabilities_curr")
liabilities	Total Liabilities	dr.GetData("liabilities")
EBITDA	Earnings Before Interest, Tax, Depreciation and Amortization	dr.GetData("EBITDA")
pref_dividends	Preferred Dividends	dr.GetData("pref_dividends")
capex_fix	Capital Expenditure on Fixed Assets	dr.GetData("capex_fix")
Capex	Capital Expenditure	dr.GetData("capex")
operating_income	Operating Income	dr.GetData("operating_income")
operating_expense	Operating Expenses	dr.GetData("operating_expense")
Cogs	Cost of Goods Sold	dr.GetData("cogs")
bookvalue_ps	Bookvalue Per Share	dr.GetData("bookvalue_ps")
return_assets	Returns on Assets	dr.GetData("return_assets")
return_equity	Returns on Equity	dr.GetData("return_equity")
inventory	Total Inventory	dr.GetData("inventory")
inventory_turnover	Quarterly Inventory Turnover	dr.GetData("inventory_turnover")

AVAILABLE OPERATORS

The operators given in Table 29.3 can be used in alpha expressions.

Table 29.3 Operators

Operator	Description	Return type
+, -, *, /, ^	Add, Subtract, Multiply, Divide, Power	Vector
<, <=, >, >=, ==, !=	Logic comparison operators	Vector
||, &&, !	Logical OR, AND, Negation	Vector
cond ? expr1 : expr2	If cond is true, expr1; else expr2. For example, close < open ? close : open	Vector
Rank(x)	Rank the values of x among all instruments, and the return values are float numbers equally distributed between 0.0 and 1.0. For example, given 6 stocks with close price [20.2, 15.6, 10.0, 5.7, 50.2, 18.4], rank(close) returns [0.8, 0.4, 0.2, 0.0, 1.0, 0.6].	Vector

(Continues)

Table 29.3   Operators   *(Continued)*

Operator	Description	Return type
Min(x, y)	Parallel minimum of vectors x and y (similar to the pmin function in R). This takes 2 vectors as arguments and returns a single vector giving the "parallel" minima of the vectors. The first element of the result is the minimum of the first elements of all the arguments, the second element of the result is the minimum of the second elements of all the arguments and so on.	Vector
Max(x, y)	Parallel maximum of vectors x and y (similar to the pmax function in R). This takes 2 vectors as arguments and returns a single vector giving the "parallel" maxima of the vectors. The first element of the result is the maximum of the first elements of both the arguments, the second element of the result is the maximum of the second elements of both the arguments and so on.	Vector
StdDev(x, n)	Standard deviation of the values in vector x for the past n days. Note that n must be less than 256.	Scalar
Correlation(x, y, n)	Correlation of the values in vectors x and y for the past n days. Note that n must be less than 256.	Scalar
Sum(x, n)	Sum of the values in vector x for the past n days. Note that n must be less than 256.	Scalar
Covariance(x, y, n)	Covariance of the values in vectors x and y for the past n days. Note that n must be less than 256.	Scalar
CountNans(x, n)	Number of NaN (Not-a-Number) values in vector x for the past n days. Note that n must be less than 256. E.g.: CountNans((close-open)^0.5, 22) If (close > open) then (close - open)^0.5 is not NaN. else if (close < open) then (close - open)^0.5 is NaN. So, basically the above code counts how many times close is less than open, in the past 22 days.	Vector

Operator	Description	Return type
Abs(x)	Absolute value	Vector
Delay(x, n)	Value of x at n days ago. Note that n must be less than 256.	Vector
Step(x)	For all instruments, current day is x, yesterday is x-1, and so on.	Vector
	Step(x) creates a vector for each instrument, whose value is x for today, x-1 for yesterday, and so on.	
	For example, Step(1250) would create the following array for each instrument:	
	[..., -3, -2, -1, 0, 1, 2, ..., 1249, 1250]	
	The last value corresponds to "today."	
	Suppose you enter expression Sum(Step(5)*close,5)	
	This would calculate:	
	5 * close[today] + 4 * close[today-1] + ... + 1 * close[today-4]	
	i.e. it calculates a sort of weighted mean of close price for last 5 days.	
Delta(x, n)	x[date] - x[date - n]. Note that n must be less than 256	Vector
Decay_linear(x, n)	Linear decay function over the past n days. $Decay\_linear(x, n) = (x[date] * n + x[date - 1] * (n - 1) + ... + x[date - n - 1]) / (n + (n - 1) + ... + 1)$	Vector
Decay_exp(x, f, n)	Exponential decay function over the past n days, where f is the smoothing factor. Here f is the smoothing factor and can be assigned a value that's less than 1. $Decay\_exp(x, f, n) = (x[date] + x[date - 1] * f + ... + x[date - n - 1] * (f \wedge (n - 1))) / (1 + f + ... + f \wedge (n - 1))$	Vector
Product(x, n)	Product of the values in vector x for the past n days $Product(x, n) = x[date] * x[date - 1] * ... * x[date - n - 1]$	Scalar
Tail(x, lower, upper, newval)	Set the values of x to newval if they are between lower and upper.	Vector
Ts_Min(x, n)	Minimum value of x over the last n days. Note that this is different than Min	Vector

(Continues)

Table 29.3   Operators   (*Continued*)

Operator	Description	Return type
Ts_Max(x, n)	Maximum value of x over the last n days. Note that this is different than Max.	Vector
Sum_i(expr, var, start, stop, step)	Loop over var (from start to stop with step) and calculate expr at every iteration (presumably expr would contain var), then sum over all the values. For example: Sum_i(Delay(close, i)*i, i, 2, 4, 1) would be equivalent to Delay(close, 2)*2 + Delay(close, 3)*3 + Delay(close, 4)*4	Scalar
Call_i(expr, var, subexpr)	Substitute subexpr for var in expr, and then evaluate expr. For example, Call_i(x + 4, x, 2 + 3) would be equivalent to (2 + 3) + 4	Vector
Sign(x)	Returns 1 if x > 0, -1 if x < 0, 0 if x == 0	Vector
SignedPower(x, e)	Sign(x) * (Abs(x)^e)	Vector
Pasteurize(x)	Pasteurize the signals. Set to NaN if it is INF or if the underlying instrument is not in the universe.	Vector
Log(x)	Natural logarithm	Vector
Ts_Rank(x, n)	Rank the values of x of the same instrument over the past n days, then return the rank of the current value. The rank value is between 0.0 ~ 1.0, as illustrated in the explanation of Rank(x).	Vector
Ts_Skewness(x, n)	Compute the skewness of x on the last n days	Scalar
Ts_Kurtosis(x, n)	Compute the kurtosis of x on the last n days.	Scalar
Ts_Moment(x, k, n)	Compute the kth central moment of x on the last n days	Scalar
IndNeutralize(x, y)	Neutralize alpha x against groupings specified by y. For example, IndNeutralize(x, industry) and IndNeutralize(x, subindustry) to neutralize against industries and subindustries respectively. To neutralize against market, use IndNeutralize(x, 1).	Vector
Scale(x)	Scale alpha x so that its Book size is 1, i.e., the sum of abs(x) over all instruments is 1. To scale to a different book size, say 1000, use Scale(x) * 1000.	Vector

Note: x and y mentioned above as function arguments are vectors. Use market data in their stead.

Also note, the value 256 here refers to the number of lookback days. For example, if the average of cps value of the past 10 days needs to be determined, for the first date of simulation window period, it needs to fetch previous 10 days close price values. Since 10 is less than the default value of 256 for lookback days, it will fetch the required values. Let's say that you are checking for average of close price for the past 257 days. Then for the first date of the simulation period, it will not be able to fetch the data for current date-257th date.

30
Interpreting Results and Alpha Repository

By the WebSim™ Team

This chapter provides an overview on different factors used to measure alpha performance, keeping track of all alphas and a list of errors and warnings from simulations.

SHARPE RATIO BRACKET

As seen in Figure 30.1, in the Simulation Results page, you will find a label just below your alpha expression and above the Cumulative Profits graph that says Spectacular, Excellent, Good, Average, Inferior, and Poor depending on your alpha's Sharpe Ratio and Fitness, as shown in Table 30.1.

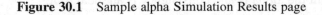

	Percentile Rank	Total Submissions	Sharpe	Return	Fitness
Excellent					
	ALL	187	100%	98%	95%
	Delay-1	187	100%	98%	95%
	US: TOP3000 Delay-1	175	100%	98%	95%

Figure 30.1 Sample alpha Simulation Results page

Table 30.1 Table to illustration Sharpe Ratio grading scale

Label	Sharpe for Delay 1 alphas	Sharpe for Delay 0 alphas
Spectacular	>4.5	>6.0
Excellent	>3.5	>5.25
Good	>3.0	>4.50
Average	> 2.5	>3.95
Inferior	>=1	>=1
Poor	<1	<1

Please note that the above categorization can be changed anytime at the firm's discretion. For the most updated definition please check WebSim™ help page.

If you click on the "+" to expand it, you will find a Percentile Rank table. The percentile ranks of current simulated alphas of historic simulations submitted by this user are:

- **ALL**: (1st row) refers to the space of all historic simulations.
- **Delay-1/0**: (2nd row) indicates the space of all historic simulations with the same delay setting.
- **USA:TOP-N Delay-1/0**: (3rd row) denotes the space of all historic simulations with the same delay and universe settings.

Percentile ranks in Sharpe, Return, and Fitness are listed in the table, respectively.

Sharpe and IR

The terms Sharpe and IR (information ratio) are used interchangeably.

The IR measures the prediction ability of a model. It refers to *the ratio of portfolio's returns above the returns of a benchmark (usually an index) to the volatility of those returns*. One could also say that it measures an alpha's ability to generate excess returns relative to a benchmark, but also attempts to identify the consistency of the alpha. This ratio will identify if the alpha has beaten the benchmark by a lot in a few months or a little every month. The higher the IR, the more consistent the alpha is and consistency is an ideal trait.

Sharpe is the annualized version of the IR statistic, i.e. **Sharpe = sqrt (252)*IR ~= 15.8*IR**; where 252 is the average number of trading days (or days the markets are open) in the USA in a year.

An alpha should have a minimum Sharpe of 3.95 for delay 0 alphas and around 2.5 for delay 1 alphas to be eligible for out-of-sample testing.

Return and Fitness

Return is the gain or loss of a security in a particular period. The Return consists of the income and the capital gains relative on an investment. **Return = Annualized PnL/Half of Book Size**. Good alphas should obviously generate high Sharpe over Returns.

Fitness of an alpha is a function of Return, Turnover, and Sharpe. Good alphas have high fitness.

SIMULATION RESULTS

Cumulative Profit graph (Figure 30.2): A graph of alpha's performance over a spread of one, three and six months, Year to Date, one year and all time. This graph can be zoomed in by clicking and dragging in the plot area. Start and end dates for PnL plotting can also be changed here. Just below the PnL graph is the Sharpe Ratio graph (Sharpe vs. Time). Make sure that the PnL graph has an upward trend, the Sharpe is high, and the Drawdown is kept to a minimum.

A summary of results is given in Figure 30.3.

Year: It is the year on which the data was simulated. The last row shows the alpha's overall performance.

Book size: Book size refers to the size of the simulation book. This means that it is the amount of capital used during the simulation to go long and short on every instrument. The Book size is constant and is set to $20 million. Therefore only $20 million is used all throughout the simulation. Profit is not reinvested and the losses are compensated by addition of cash.

WebSim™ assumes you have $10 million and will invest in assets up to $20 million. This is called leverage. Performance (like Returns, Sharpe) is computed on a base of $10 million.

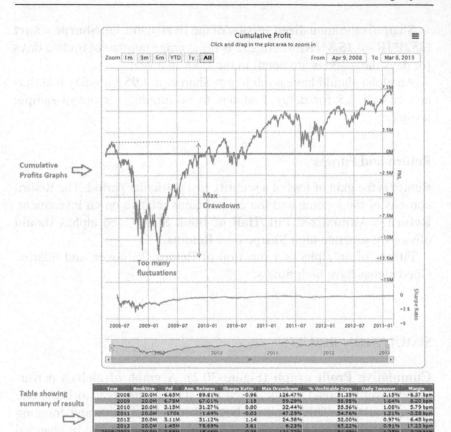

Figure 30.2   Cumulative Profit graph

Year	Booksize	Pnl	Ann. return	Sharpe ratio	Max drawdown	% profitable days	Daily turnover	Profit per $ traded
2008	2.0E7	1.66E6	21.47%	3.10	2.76%	58.03%	40.12%	0.11 ¢
2009	2.0E7	2.42E6	24.03%	5.12	1.70%	60.32%	38.56%	0.12 ¢
2010	2.0E7	1.33E6	13.15%	4.20	2.04%	60.71%	38.65%	0.07 ¢
2011	2.0E7	1.28E6	12.67%	3.27	3.46%	56.35%	39.05%	0.06 ¢
2012	2.0E7	1.18E6	11.84%	4.53	0.66%	62.00%	39.15%	0.06 ¢
2013	2.0E7	89.71E3	4.88%	2.19	0.50%	56.52%	37.40%	0.03 ¢
2008 - 2013	2.0E7	7.96E6	15.98%	3.71	3.46%	59.44%	39.00%	0.08 ¢

Figure 30.3 A summary of alpha simulation results

PnL: Profit and Loss (aka PnL) is the money that the positions and trades generate (which means it is the amount of money you lost or made during the year), expressed in dollars.

$$daily\_PnL = sum\ of\ (position * daily\_return)$$

Daily return here is per instrument (today's close/yesterday's close) − 1.0.

Annual Return: It is the return on capital used. **Annual Return = Annualized PnL/Half of Book Size.** It signifies the amount you made or lost during the period observed and is expressed in %.

Max Drawdown: It is the percentage of largest loss against half of Book size divided by the maximal negative series from daily PnL. One can also say that it is the absolute value of maximum peak to trough return. It signifies the low point of the PnL (maximum loss of money) for the period observed.

Sharpe: **Sharpe = Avg(return)/Std_dev(return)** over the observed time period.

% Profitable Days: It is the ratio between positive PnL days divided and number of days traded.

Daily Turnover: It signifies how often one trades. It can be defined as the ratio of the value traded over the shares held. **Daily Turnover = Trading_volume/2 * Size.** Good alphas have low turnover.

Profit per $ Traded: It measures how profitable your trades are. **Profit per $ Traded = PnL/dollars traded.** This number doesn't factor in cost of trading.

MY ALPHAS PAGE

Figure 30.4 shows a summary of the expressions simulated so far.
   The controls available on this page are:

- **Favorite**: Alphas can be marked as favorite by selecting them using the checkbox and clicking the α button on the top right corner. The same procedure on favorite alphas allows to un-favorite an alpha. The current status of an alpha is shown by the α next to it.
- **Delete**: Alphas can be deleted by selecting them using the checkbox and clicking the 🗑 button on the top right corner.

My Alphas

In-Sample | Out-Sample

Show / hide filters

Show 20 ▼ entries
Showing 1 to 20 of 183 entries

Name	Created	Simulation Duration	Universe	Decay	Delay	Neutralization	Truncation	Sharpe	Returns	PnL	Turnover	Drawdown	Margin
021014064011	2014-02-10 06:40:34	5	US: TOP3000	0	1	none	0	3.4	10.33%	4.77M	33.61%	3.46%	0.05 bpm
021714085657	2014-02-17 08:57:08	5	US: TOP3000	1	1	market	0	2.75	12.09%	5.86M	45.87%	3.32%	0.06 bpm
021714090408	2014-02-17 09:04:19	5	US: TOP3000	1	1	market	0	2.69	14%	6.46M	45.7%	4.34%	0.06 bpm
021714090506	2014-02-17 09:05:17	5	US: TOP3000	5	1	market	0	2.63	13.75%	6.33M	34.34%	4.25%	0.08 bpm
021114090116	2014-02-11 09:01:21	5	US: TOP3000	0	1	market	0	2.6	13.56%	6.25M	40.97%	4.46%	0.07 bpm
020914064019	2014-02-09 06:40:40	5	US: TOP3000	5	1	none	0	2.49	14.37%	6.64M	46.12%	5.18%	0.06 bpm
021014064423	2014-02-10 06:44:45	5	US: TOP3000	0	1	none	0	2.48	13.7%	6.33M	36.41%	5.1%	0.08 bpm
020914063115	2014-02-09 06:31:15	5	US: TOP3000	5	1	subindustry	0	2.48	14.29%	6.6M	48.13%	5.14%	0.06 bpm

First Previous 1 2 3 4 5 Next Last

Figure 30.4 A summary of the simulated expressions

- **Filters**: Filters can be used to view a subset of all alphas. The various parameters by which you can filter are – Name (regex allowed), Universe, Decay, Sharpe, Turnover, Rating, Code, Simulation Duration, Neutralization, Returns, Drawdown, Date Created, Delay, Truncation, PnL, and Margin. *[Note: Margin is the PnL divided by dollars traded. It is the same as the "Profit per $ Traded" column on the results page. The unit bpm stands for Basis points (margin)]*
- **Number of Entries**: To restrict the number of entries shown on a page use the **Show N Entries** dropdown menu. You can then navigate between pages using the **Previous/Next** buttons or the numbered buttons.
- **View Code/Simulation**: Hover over the 🟢 button to view the code for an expression. You can them click the 🔘 button to simulate the expression and view detailed results.
- **Sorting**: The table is sortable by each of the displayed columns. Click on the column header to cycle between Increasing and Decreasing order of sorting.

In-Sample – This section has a summary of the performance of alphas up to the date on which they were first simulated, i.e. in-sample performance of an alpha is the performance obtained from backtesting on historical data. This is the performance you see on the results page when simulating an alpha. The data displayed for these alphas are: Name, Date Created, Simulation Duration, Universe, Decay, Delay, Neutralization, Truncation, Sharpe, Returns, PnL, Drawdown, and Margin.

Out-Sample – *An alpha should have a minimum Sharpe of 3.95 for delay 0 alphas, and around 2.5 for delay 1 alphas to be eligible for out-of-sample testing.* Out-sample performance of an alpha is the performance after its date of submission. It is the "real world" performance on alpha. The "Out-Sample" tab shows the Sharpe (performance) of an alpha over various time periods like 30 days, 40 days, 60 days to a year. For selected alphas we run out-sample simulations; the results are shown in Figure 30.5. The data displayed for these alphas are: Name, Test Date, Sharpe over various periods (e.g. Sharpe30 is for one month and Sharpe360 is for a year), Total Out Sample Sharpe, Correlation Stats (with your own alphas, threshold being 0.5 to 0.7), and Rating (on a scale from 0 to 100). Sharpe over various periods

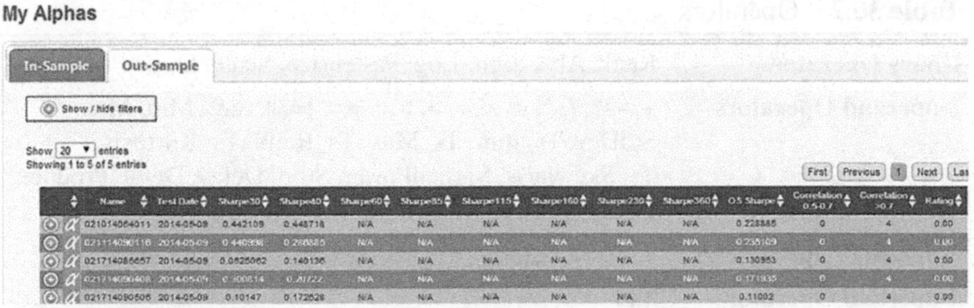

My Alphas

In-Sample | Out-Sample

Show / hide filters

Show 20 entries
Showing 1 to 5 of 5 entries

First Previous 1 Next Las

Name	Test Date	Sharpe30	Sharpe40	Sharpe60	Sharpe85	Sharpe115	Sharpe160	Sharpe230	Sharpe360	OS Sharpe	Correlation 0.5-0.7	Correlation >0.7	Rating
021014064011	2014-05-09	0.442109	0.448718	N/A	N/A	N/A	N/A	N/A	N/A	0.228885	0	4	0.00
021114090116	2014-05-09	0.440936	0.286885	N/A	N/A	N/A	N/A	N/A	N/A	0.235109	0	4	0.00
021714086657	2014-05-09	0.0825062	0.140136	N/A	N/A	N/A	N/A	N/A	N/A	0.130953	0	4	0.00
021714090408	2014-05-09	0.300614	0.20722	N/A	N/A	N/A	N/A	N/A	N/A	0.171935	0	4	0.00
021714090506	2014-05-09	0.10147	0.172628	N/A	N/A	N/A	N/A	N/A	N/A	0.11002	0	4	0.00

Figure 30.5 Out-Sample Sharpe Ratio over various time periods

allows you to keep track of out-sample performance of your alpha (Figure 30.5).

Correlation: It is important to understand the idea of correlation. We already have thousands of alphas. If your alpha's correlations with existing models are too high (>0.7, for example), your model will probably not add value. From the correlation you can also understand the nature and category of your alphas.

So far, the entire extent of the "OS Test" for WebSim™ alphas has been the computation of correlation among themselves and with the internal pool, alpha ratings based on IS and OS performance, and OS Sharpe values.

The SharpeX field indicates the OS Sharpe of the alpha as seen over the X days starting from the first new high attained by the alpha's PnL since the day it was put into OS Test.

ERRORS AND WARNINGS

Errors and warnings include:

1. Syntax error in expression:

   Please make sure that your expression is logical. The list of tokens (operators and keywords) and numbers (0–9) shown in Tables 30.2 and 30.3 are allowed in your alpha expression.
2. Cannot retrieve simulation status:

   This is seen if communication between our servers has temporarily broken down. This message does not relate to anything the user did.

Table 30.2 Operators

Unary Operators	Rank, Abs, Sign, Log, Pasteurize, Scale, Step
2-operand Operators	+, -, *, /, ^, <, <,=, >, >,=, ==, !=, ||, &&, Min, Max, StdDev, Ts_min, Ts_Max, Ts_Rank ,Ts_Kurtosis, Ts_Skewness, SignedPower, Sum, Delay, Delta, Product, Decay_linear, CountNans
3-operand Operators	?:, Correlation, Call_i, Ts_Moment, Decay_exp
4-operand Operator	Tail
5-operand Operator	Sum_i

3. Error simulating alpha:

This is seen when a syntax error or a runtime error is encountered in Python mode.

4. Simulation terminated due to Python security breach (e.g. enter "import sys" into the Python area and submit):

Error: Simulation terminated due to Python security breach: "Forbidden to import sys."

This is seen when forbidden actions attempted in Python code force WebSim™ to block the simulation. Such actions include attempts to open and close files, and importing restricted packages like "os," etc., which are not required for the purpose of alpha development on WebSim™.

5. Outstanding submissions:

Error: "You have an outstanding submission, please wait 572 seconds to finish."

Table 30.3 Data Fields

Price Volume Data Fields	Open, close, high, low, volume, returns, adv20, sharesout, vwap, opening
Fundamental Data Fields	sales, sales_growth, sales_ps, income, eps, cashflow, cashflow_sales, cashflow_op, cashflow_fin, cashflow_invst, inventory, assets, assets_curr, equity, debt, debt_lt, debt_st, liabilities, liabilities_curr, EBITDA, pref_dividends, cashflow_dividends, capex, capex_fix, operating_income, operating_expense, cogs, bookvalue_ps, return_assets, return_equity, inventory, inventory_turnover

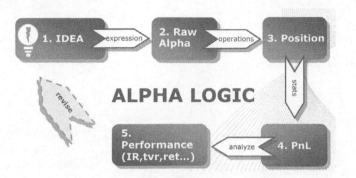

Figure 30.6   The life-cycle of an alpha

This error occurs when you submit an expression/Python code when another simulation is currently running simultaneously. To skip the waiting period, you must log out and log back into WebSim™.

QUICK RECAP

The flow chart in Figure 30.6 shows the life-cycle of an alpha.

First, one has to peruse blogs, journal, and research papers on the internet to come up with an idea. The alpha expression is entered in WebSim™, and operations (like Truncation, Neutralization, Decay) are performed on the raw alpha. WebSim™ simulates investments (goes long or short) for all the instruments of the Universe chosen in the Settings panel and the PnL is generated. Then the performance is calculated (Sharpe, Turnover, Returns) as seen in the Simulation Results page. And if the alpha is not deemed worthy, the alpha idea is revised. The cycle continues until the alpha is fit for production.

31
Alpha Tutorials
By the WebSim™ Team

This chapter provides a selection of expression and python examples to get a new user started. It also has descriptions of some common alpha examples with a discussion on good practices to follow when building alphas.

ALPHA EXPRESSION EXAMPLES

Try the alpha expressions in Table 31.1 with different Universe, Delay, Neutralization, etc. settings.

Table 31.1 Sample alpha expressions

Expression	Description
1/close	Use inverse of daily *close* price as stock weights. More allocation of capital on the stocks with lower daily *close* prices. Similarly in the examples below, more allocation of capital on stocks with higher weights as defined in the "Expression" column.
volume/adv20	Use relative *daily volume* to the *average in the past 20 days* as stock weights.
Correlation(close, open, 10)	Use *correlation* between daily *close* and *open* prices in the past 10 days as stock weights.
open	Use daily *open* price as stock weights.

(continued)

Table 31.1 (*Continued*)

Expression	Description
(high + low)/2 - close	Use difference between average of daily *high* and *low* prices and daily *close* price as stock weights.
vwap < close ? high : low	Use daily *high* as stock weights if the stock *close*s higher than daily volume weighted average price (*vwap*), or otherwise use daily *low* as stock weights.
Rank(adv20)	Use rank of average daily volume in past 20 days (*adv20*) as stock weights.
Min(0.5*(open+close), vwap)	Use the less of *open close* average and *vwap* as stock weights.
Max(0.5*(high+low), vwap)	Use the greater of *high low* average and *vwap* as stock weights.
1/StdDev(returns, 22)	Use inverse of standard deviation of stock *returns* in past 22 days as stock weights.
Sum(sharesout, 5)	Use sum of *outstanding shares* in past 5 days as stock weights.
Covariance(vwap, returns, 22)	Use covariance of *vwap* and *returns* for the past 22 days as stock weights.
1/Abs(0.5*(open+close) - vwap)	Use absolute difference between *open close* average and *vwap* as stock weights.
Correlation(vwap, Delay(close, 1), 5)	Use correlation between *vwap* and previous day's *close* for past 5 days as stock weights.
Delta(close, 5)	Use difference between daily *close* and *close* on the date 5 days earlier as stock weights.
Decay_ linear(sharesout*vwap, 5)	Use linear decay of *vwap* multiplied by *sharesout* over the last 5 days as stock weights.
Decay_exp(close, 0.25, 5)	Use exponential decay of *close* with smoothing factor 0.25 over the last 5 days as stock weights.
Product(volume/ sharesout, 5)	Use product of *volume/sharesout* ratio for the past 5 days as stock weights.
Tail(close/vwap, 0.9, 1.1, 1.0)	Use *close/vwap* ratio as stock weights if it is less than 0.9 or greater than 1.1, or otherwise use 1 as stock weights.
Sign(close-vwap)	Use 1 if *close-vwap* is positive or otherwise -1 as stock weights.
SignedPower (close-open, 0.5)	Use sqrt of absolute difference between *close* and *open* as stock weights.
Pasteurize(1/(close-open))	Use inverse of *close-open* pasteurized (set to NaN if it is INF or if the underlying instrument is not in the universe) as stock weights.

Expression	Description
Log(high/low)	Use natural logarithm of *high/low* ratio as stock weights.
IndNeutralize (volume*vwap, 1)	Use market neutralized *volume*vwap* product as stock weights.
Scale(close^0.5)	Use scaled sqrt of *close* (scaled such that the Book size is 1) as stock weights.
Ts_Min(open, 22)	Use minimum *open* over the last 22 days as stock weights.
Ts_Max(close, 22)	Use maximum *open* over the last 22 days as stock weights.
Ts_Rank(volume, 22)	Use rank of current *volume* over the past 22 days as stock weights.
Ts_Skewness(returns, 11)	Use skewness of *returns* over the last 11 days as stock weights.
Ts_Kurtosis(returns, 11)	Use kurtosis of *returns* over the last 11 days as stock weights.
Ts_Moment(returns, 3, 11)	Use 3rd central moment of *returns* over the last 11 days as stock weights.
CountNans((close-open)^0.5, 22)	Use number of NaN values in $(close-open)^{0.5}$ for the past 22 days as stock weights.
Step(1250)*close	Use *close**Step(1250) product as stock weights.
Sum_i(Delta(close,i), i,4,6,2)	Use summation of Delta(*close*,i) over i from 4 to 6 step 2 as stock weights.
Call_i(Ts_Rank(x,5),x, close>vwap ? close : high)	Use Ts_Rank(x,5) as stock weights where x is daily *close* price if it's higher than *vwap*, or otherwise use daily *high* price as stock weights.

HOW TO CODE ALPHAS IN PYTHON

You should have good working knowledge of Python programming language to develop Python alphas on WebSim™. Useful links to online Python tutorials are given in Table 31.2.

The user should abide by the terms of use of the above-mentioned sites. The links are listed for user's convenience only.

Table 31.2   Links to online Python tutorials

Quick guide for complete beginners	Language reference	Python Numerical Computation Libraries
Python Quick Guide (http://www.tutorialspoint.com/python/python_quick_guide.htm)	**Dive into Python** (http://www.diveintopython.net/)	**NumPy Official Documentation** (http://www.numpy.org/)
Hands on Python – A Tutorial for Beginners (http://www.nervenet.org/pdf/python3handson.pdf)	**Python Version 2.6.6 Documentation** (http://docs.python.org/release/2.6.6/)	**SciPy Official Documentation** (http://www.scipy.org/)
Codecademy – Learn Python with Examples (http://www.codecademy.com/tracks/python)	**Text Processing in Python** (http://gnosis.cx/TPiP/)	**NumPy Reference Guide** (http://docs.scipy.org/doc/numpy/reference/)
Fast Lane to Python – Norm Matloff (http://heather.cs.ucdavis.edu/~matloff/Python/PLN/FastLanePython.pdf)	**A Byte of Python** (http://files.swaroopch.com/python/byte_of_python_v192.pdf)	**NumPy User Guide** (http://docs.scipy.org/doc/numpy/user/)
Hands on Python Tutorial – Andrew Harrington (http://anh.cs.luc.edu/python/hands-on/index26.html)	**Think Python: How to Think Like a Computer Scientist, by Allen B. Downey** (http://www.greenteapress.com/thinkpython/)	**An Intro to NumPy and SciPy** (http://www.engr.ucsb.edu/~shell/che210d/numpy.pdf)
A Mini Python Tutorial (http://www.decalage.info/files/mini_python_tutorial_0.03.pdf)	**Quick Reference** (http://www2-pcmdi.llnl.gov/cdat/manuals/Python 2.4 Quick Reference Card.pdf)	**Scientific Python** (https://sourcesup.renater.fr/projects/scientific-py/)

Imported Libraries

Keep in mind that any user-submitted Python code is always prefixed by WebSim™ with the following:

```
import scipy as sp # python library that supplements numeric modules
from numpy import * # library that contains N-dim array object, linear
    algebra, etc.
import scipy.stats as ss # import statistical functions
delay = 1 # alpha delay
dr = WQSim_DataRegistry.Instance() # dr is initialized as data registry
    object
# use dr.GetData() to access market data
```

valid = dr.GetData_m_b("USA:TOP3000") # GetData_m_b() accesses Universe data. The result valid is a matrix of Boolean values that specifies which instruments are valid in the universe on a given day. The GetData_m_b() function is used to access data of type Boolean matrix(_m_b stands for matrix, boolean)

Accessing Data

WebSim™ application is enabled to access market data on the back end by using the Python code, GetDataon, the data registry. For example:

shares_outstanding=dr.GetData("sharesout") # to access outstanding shares data
ltDebt=dr.GetData("debt_lt") # for long-term debt data
closePrice=dr.GetData("close") # for close price data

Generate() Function, Indices, and Alpha Expression

As explained before, the market data can be thought of as a matrix of values provided for each stock for every date the data is made available. The dates are mapped to date indices di and the instruments are mapped to instrument indices ii as shown in Table 31.3.

Table 31.3 Mapping dates to date indices di and instruments to instrument indices ii

Dates	di(date index)	Instruments	ii(instr index)
20100101	0	MSFT	0
20100102	1	AAPL	1
20100103	2	PG	2
20100104	3	GOOG	3
20100107	4	AA	4
20100108	5	K	5
...	...	...	...

Market data, e.g. close price, would be arranged in the form of a matrix as shown in Table 31.4.

Now to access Apple's close price on date Jan 7, 2010, we need to use close(3,2).

Table 31.4 Market data arranged in the form of a matrix

Instruments Dates	MSFT (ii=0)	HOG (ii=1)	AAPL (ii=2)	GOOG (ii=3)	PG (ii=4)	
20100104(di=0)	30.95	25.46	214.01	626.75	61.12	...
20100105(di=1)	30.96	25.65	214.38	623.99	61.14	...
20100106(di=2)	30.77	25.59	210.97	608.26	60.85	...
20100107(di=3)	30.452	25.8	210.58	594.1	60.52	...
20100108(di=4)	30.66	25.53	211.98	602.02	60.44	...
...	...	...	...	...	...	...

The sole purpose of the Generate( ) function (should be implemented in your code) is to populate the resulting alpha vector with stock
weights for every stock. The Generate function will evaluate the alpha
expression for every date (it acts like a loop that iterates through all
date indices), hence its arguments are di (which is the date index corresponding to the current date) and alpha (the resulting vector that needs
to be filled). For example:

```
closePrice = dr.GetData("close")
def Generate(di,alpha):
# Alpha expression goes here
```

Data can be accessed using dataname[di-delay,ii].
dataName[date index, instrument index] would give you the value
of dataname, for that particular date, and that particular instrument.
To assign expression to an alpha, use alpha[instrument index] =
expression.
For example, alpha[ii] = dataname[di,ii].
An example alpha code to use close price data is given below:

```
closePrice = dr.GetData("close")
def Generate(di,alpha):
alpha[:] = 1./closePrice[di-delay,:]
# The above statement is equivalent to the expression '1/close'
# ":" here refers to all instrument indices 0 <= ii< alpha.shape[0]
```

Since we are using the list-slicing functionality (":") of Python, it
executes the expression for each instrument (corresponding column cell
in the matrix).

Another example that uses returns data to define alpha[:] is given below:

```
returnsMat = dr.GetData("returns")
def Generate(di,alpha):
alpha[:] = -(returnsMat[di-delay,:]) # reversion(returns always tends to
    mean)
```

To access data for an instrument over a certain window period, say n days, use dataname[di-delay-n: di-delay, ii]. An example for this is given below:

```
closePrice = dr.GetData("close")
def Generate(di,alpha):
alpha[:] = mean(close[di-delay-10:di-delay,:], axis = 0) # taking the
    mean of the close price for the last 10 days
alpha[:] = where(valid[di,:],alpha[:],nan) # valid check
```

The user should note that the window period chosen should be less that the number of lookback days (namely set to 256 days, by default). This value can be retrieved using Python function: Build.GetBackdays().

The last line is added as a validity check for values in the resultant alpha array. This will ensure that the values for instruments that don't belong to the TOP3000 universe will be filtered out. Notice that this uses the valid variable, which was initialized as mentioned in the Python code header. This is explained further in the next section.

PYTHON ALPHA EXAMPLES

Here are several common examples of how Python can be used.

Using Multiple Data Simultaneously

The following example shows us how to access and use multiple data at the same time. Use vectorization wherever possible. Avoid using loops as they are slow. This example uses NumPy's built-in math function (numpy.subtract is called automatically). Here, the alpha vector is assigned expression close – high.

```
# Different data need different variables
closePrice=dr.GetData("close")
highPrice=dr.GetData("high")
def Generate(di,alpha):
alpha[:] = closePrice[di-delay,:] - highPrice[di-delay,:]
```

Using Custom-Defined Functions

The following py code shows us how to define custom functions and use them. It also uses the NumPy function numpy.where(). This should be used instead of loops to perform vector comparison.

```
closePrice=dr.GetData("close")
lowPrice=dr.GetData("low")
def Generate(di,alpha):
# np_max (defined below) can be called in this code
alpha[:] = np_max(closePrice[di-delay,:], lowPrice[di-delay-1, :])
# This is equivalent to the expression 'Max(close, Delay(low, 1))'
def np_max(data1, data2):
return where(data1 > data2, data1, data2) # numpy.where() performs
   vector comparison
```

Incorrect Way to Assign Alpha Values

```
closePrice=dr.GetData("close")
def Generate(di,alpha):
alpha[:] = closePrice[di-delay,:] # equivalent to the expression 'close'
alpha = ones(alpha.shape[0])
# Tries to assign all ones to the alpha vector using numpy.ones
# Notice the lack of [:] after "alpha." This assigns a new object to
   alpha rather than modify the existing object alpha is pointing to.
   The effect of this statement is that WebSim™ loses track of the
   alpha vector
alpha[:]=1./closePrice[di-delay,:] # equivalent to the expression "1/close"
# This statement has no effect because of the statement before it. The
   final alpha value is "close" instead of "1/close"
```

Use of Valid Matrix

The valid matrix has a list of valid instruments (for example, 3,000 instruments for TOP3000) and is automatically available:

```
closePrice=dr.GetData("close")
def Generate(di,alpha):
alpha[:] = 1./closePrice[di-delay,:]
alpha[:] = onlyValid(alpha, di) # User defined function. Filters out values for invalid instruments
def onlyValid(x, di):
myValid = valid[di-delay, :] # myValid vector has yesterday's valid values only
return where(myValid, x, nan)
# We use NumPy's where() function to filter out invalid instruments
    Always assign numpy.nan() to filter out instruments. "0" is a valid alpha value
```

The above valid-check function can be inserted at the end of all your alpha codes as:

```
alpha[:] = where(valid[di-delay,:],alpha[:],nan)
```

Using Statistics Functions Available in SciPy

A list of SciPy's statistical functions can be found at SciPy.org. We will be using the scipy .rankdata() function here. This assigns ranks to alpha weight, dealing with ties appropriately.

```
high=dr.GetData("high")
def Generate(di,alpha):
alpha[:] = ss.rankdata(high[di-delay, :]) # using SciPy's rank function.
    The equivalent expression is Rank(high)
alpha[:] = where(valid[di-delay,:],alpha[:],nan)
```

The above alpha expression ranks (on a scale from 0 to 1) adjusted High prices.

The following alpha example shows the usage of a SciPy function called scipy.kurtosis() on close price for 11 days.

```
closePrice = dr.GetData("close")
def Generate(di,alpha):
alpha[:]  =  ss.kurtosis(close[di-delay-11:di-delay,:],  axis  =  0)  #
    using SciPy's kurtosis function. The equivalent expression is
    kurtosis(close,11)
alpha[:] = where(valid[di-delay,:],alpha[:],nan)
```

The following alpha example shows the usage of a SciPy function called scipy.skewness() on returns for 10 days.

```
returns = dr.GetData("returns")
def Generate(di, alpha):
alpha[:]  =  ss.skew (returns[di-delay-10:di-delay,:],  axis  =  0)  #
    using SciPy's skewness function. The expression is equivalent to
    skewness(returns,10)
alpha[:] = where(valid[di-delay,:],alpha[:],nan)
```

Using Statistics Functions Available in NumPy

A list of NumPy's statistical functions can be found here: NumPy.org.
The alpha example below shows usage of NumPy's mean and standard deviation function numpy.std():

```
closePrice = dr.GetData("close")
def Generate(di,alpha):
alpha[:]  =  mean(close[di-delay-5:di-delay,:],  axis  =  0)/std(close[di-
    delay-5:di-delay,:], axis = 0)
# equivalent to expression [Sum(close,5)/5]/ StdDev(close,5)
alpha[:] = where(valid[di,:],alpha[:],nan)
```

The alpha example below shows usage of NumPy's maximum function numpy.amax():

```
closePrice = dr.GetData("close")
def Generate(di, alpha):
alpha[:] = amax(close[di-delay-20:di-delay,:], axis = 0) # finds maxi-
    mum close over past 20 days
alpha[:] = where(valid[di,:],alpha[:],nan)
```

Accessing and Using Industry Data

```
closePrice = dr.GetData("close")
industry = dr.GetData("industry") # accessing industry data
def Generate(di,ti,alpha):
ind = unique(where(industry[di-delay, :] > 0, industry[di-delay, :], 0))
indclose = zeros(ind.shape[0]) # initialize a NumPy array full of zeros
for i in xrange(ind.shape[0]):
indclose[i] = mean(where((industry[di-delay, :] == ind[i]) * (valid[di-
    delay, :]), closePrice[di-delay, :], 0))
alpha[:] = where( (industry[di-delay, :] == ind[i]) * (valid[di-delay,:]),
    indclose[i], alpha[:])
```

Industry data here is a NumPy array of indices assigned for every available industry. Industries such as Forestry, Metal Mining, Electrical Work, Meat Packing Plants, Textile Mills, Book Printing, etc., have indices assigned to them. The alpha above shows how this industry data can be accessed and used.

Table 31.5 shows a sample of instrument indices, industry indices (values of industry[di-delay,ii]), close data.

Table 31.5 Sample instrument indices, industry indices (values of industry [di-delay, ii], close data

ii	industry[di-delay,ii]	close[di-delay,ii]
0	2	1.0
1	1	-2.0
2	0 ⟶	5.0
3	1	-3.0
4	1	-4.0
5	2	5.0
6	0 ⟶	2.0

For the above alpha example, the industry close array values for each "I" will be as follows:

Since indclose[i] = Average of closePrice[di-delay,ii] if current instrument belongs to current industry,
indclose[0] = (5.0+2.0)/2 = 3.5 (shown in table)
indclose[1] = (-2.0-3.0-4.0)/3 = -3
indclose[2] = (1.0+5.0)/2 = 3
Then alpha[ii] is assigned the value of indclose[industry[di-delay,ii]]

Note that you can also access and use sector and subindustry data using dr.GetData() in your alphas.

Simple Linear Regression Model

In the code given below, five days' values of close price and vwap as training sample are used to calculate regression weights w1 and w2.

Model formula: close[di] = w1 * close[di-1] + w2* vwap[di-1]

```
closePrice=dr.GetData("close")
vwapPrice=dr.GetData("vwap")
def Generate(di,alpha):
CloseX=zeros((5,closePrice.shape[1])) # initialize NumPy array
CloseY=zeros((5,closePrice.shape[1]))
VwapX=zeros((5,vwapPrice.shape[1]))
for dnum in xrange(5):
CloseX[dnum,:]=closePrice[di-delay-dnum-1,:]
VwapX[dnum,:]=vwapPrice[di-delay-dnum-1,:]
CloseY[dnum,:]= closePrice[di-delay-dnum,:]
for ii in xrange(alpha.shape[0]):
SampleX=hstack((CloseX[:,[ii]],VwapX[:,[ii]])) # NumPy function
   hstack() stacks arrays in sequence horizontally(column wise)
ParaX=LinearRegres(SampleX,CloseY[:,[ii]])
alpha[ii]=float(ParaX[0])*closePrice[di-delay,ii]+float(ParaX[1])
   *vwapPrice[di-delay,ii] # equivalent to expression: w1 * close[di-1]
   + w2* vwap[di-1]
alpha[:] = where(valid[di,:],alpha[:],nan)
def LinearRegres(xArr,yArr):
xMat=matrix(xArr)
yMat=matrix(yArr)
xTx= xMat.T*xMat
res=linalg.det(xTx) # NumPy's linear algebra function that computes
   the determinant of the array
if res==0.0 or isnan(res): # if res is 0 or nan
return matrix([[nan],[nan]])
else:
return xTx.I*(xMat.T*yMat) # matrix.I takes the matrix's inverse and
   matrix.T takes its transpose.
```

32
FAQs

By the WebSim™ Team

This chapter has a collection of questions that have arisen from the WebSim™ user community.

WebSim™

1. Does WebSim™ work with every browser?

    Answer: Officially supported desktop browsers:
    - Internet Explorer 9 and above
    - Firefox 3.6 and above
    - Chrome

    Safari 5.1 and above, and most versions of Opera, while not officially supported, may work fairly well. All desktop OSs that can run a supported browser are supported. There is partial support for mobile devices including Android and iOS (no guarantees here).

2. Is it possible to submit many alphas at the same time?

    Answer: It is not possible to submit many alphas in the same session. But with multiple sessions you can have one running in each simultaneously. You can do this by being logged in from multiple browsers/machines.

3. How do you get each stock position from the expression result?

    Answer: Figure 32.1 shows the sequence of operations/ transformations that are applied on an alpha.

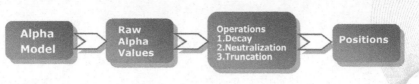

Figure 32.1   The sequence of operations/transformations that are applied
on an alpha

4. I feel there are limited financial ratios, EBITDA, ROE, ROA, etc. Is there any other financial ratio provided, or do we have to calculate it by ourselves?

Answer: All the data series that are available currently are listed on the FAQ page. More are going to be released in the coming months.

5. I accidently double clicked the submit button, and got an error message saying "You have an outstanding submission, please wait 599 seconds to finish." I am wondering if it is possible to abort a running simulation.

Answer: No. Currently, one cannot abort a running simulation. You can, however, logout from the session and log back in. This would stop your ongoing simulation. You can also use the "Escape" key. We are working on adding an abort button to our simulation window.

6. When I type into the expression box, I see some suggestions. Do they come from my own history or from all users' history?

Answer: The suggestions come from the user's own history.

7. Can you give meaningful names to your alphas?

Answer: Yes, you can give meaningful names to your alphas. You need to go to the My Alphas page and click on the alpha Id to rename it.

8. Can you group "logically similar" alphas together in the My Alphas table? Currently you can sort by Date Created and some other fields, but I want to be able to indicate that a given group of expressions are different versions of the same basic idea and group them together for visual clarity.

Answer: No, it is not apparent how alphas are logically similar. Yes, it would be useful to use other classifications to group alphas other than grouping them by date and this warrants more study.

9. Why am I getting stuck on the simulation progress page at the "Initiating…" stage? And why isn't the Python code being syntax highlighted in code input box?

Answer: Both these problems can be fixed by Enabling JavaScript in your browser settings.

10. I'm facing issues while registering with WebSim™. Who should I contact?

Answer: A list of common issues users report, and the likely cause and fix, is shown in Table 32.1 and should help in most cases.

Note: Third party links mentioned above are for user's convenience only. User should read and abide by terms of use of these sites.

If your issue doesn't get resolved using the above table, please send us an email through the WebSim™ contact page (https://websim .worldquantchallenge.com/contact).

11. Where is my profile? How can I change my password?

Answer: You can view your profile at My Account (https://wqwebres .mlp.com:9104/edit_account.html) and change your password at Change Password (https://wqwebres.mlp.com:9104/change_password .html).

12. I wonder what's the underlying of the return variable for the alpha expression? I mean, which stock's return is THE RETURN? By the

Table 32.1 Common issues reported by users and the likely cause and fixes

Known issues	Likely cause	Fix
While trying to sign up, clicking I Agree on Agreement page sends me back to the Welcome page.	Cookies are disabled	Enable cookies in browser settings (http://www.wikihow .com/Enable-Cookies-in-Your-Internet-Web-Browser)
User did not receive account confirmation email	Email provider marked our email as spam, or user-defined filters placed it in an infrequently checked subfolder of their inbox	1. Check spam folder and any subfolders inside inbox. 2. If this doesn't help, use one of the popular web-based email providers (e.g. Gmail, Yahoo).
No syntax highlighting in code input box	Javascript disabled	Enable JavaScript in browser settings (http://www.wikihow .com/Enable-JavaScript-on-Your-Computer).

way, is there any way to change the default underlying asset? Say I want use my alpha to trade hi-tech companies like Google and Apple, but not retail companies like Walmart.

Answer: WebSim™ doesn't calculate returns for individual stocks or a user-defined subset of instruments (stocks/contracts). Instead it calculates returns for a universe of liquid instruments. WebSim™ gives you the option to choose from different universes (please read the FAQ for more details). For example, if you choose USTOP3000 stocks, WebSim™ will evaluate the expression for the top 3,000 liquid stocks in the US region. Unfortunately, you cannot work with a subset of the universe or specify the industry/sub-industry. All you can do in this case is change the Universe settings using the Settings panel.

This is done by WebSim™ to ensure that you make a robust alpha model that is not biased to some stocks. This is a method of ensuring that your alpha is market/industry/sub-industry neutralized.

13. Can the author add tags/notes (maybe name simulations instead of numbers) to each simulation in "My Alphas" page? It will be very useful to search for alphas. For example, one could use a tag name #factor. One can simply try these factors by copying them instead of typing every time. If this facility is already available, please let me know.

Answer: Thanks for your good suggestion. Currently, the name region of each alpha can be editable if you click it. Please try to rename your alpha. Filters can be used by name parameter, so you can search the alpha easily.

ALPHA EXPRESSIONS, MARKET DATA, AND FUNCTIONS

1. What does -1*alpha imply?
   Answer: The final alpha values (after neutralization, etc.) indicate what proportions of the investment pool should be used to go long on (for +ve values) or short on (−ve values) various tickers. Thus, it is fairly straightforward to figure out how various manipulations will affect alpha weights. -1*alpha would use the exact same amount of capital to go long on a ticker as alpha would use to go short on the same ticker.
2. Is there any existing function to implement moving average calculation?
   Answer: Sum, Sum_i and Call_i among others can be used to construct various moving averages. To calculate exponential moving average, please use the decay_exp(x,f,n) function.

3. What does NaN mean? Is it equal to zero?

   Answer: NaN stands for Not a Number. It is used to indicate results of "invalid" operations like division by zero or if some data is corrupt or unavailable. If alpha = NaN for some stock, then it means no position is taken on that stock. While if alpha = 0 for some stock, then after operations like decay, neutralization, etc., alpha may have a non-zero value, resulting in some position being taken on the stock. In a variety of situations, if there is no alpha value for an instrument, the alpha is set to NaN. For example, if there is bad or missing data, the value is set to invalid.

4. How often does the data cache get refreshed?

   Answer: The data gets refreshed every week. Once it is refreshed, you will be able to work with the most recently available data.

5. How do I define global variables in Python code? I would like to use global var, which will be saved a value and changed every day.

   Answer: An example code on how to define and use global variables is given below:
   closePrice = dr.GetData("close")
   Var = 1 # global variable initialization
   def Generate(di,alpha):
   global Var # accessing from within the function
   wdi1 = (di-delay)%closePrice.shape[0]
   wdi2 = (di-delay-3)%closePrice.shape[0]
   if **Var > 0:**
   Var += 1 # Using it
   # some more operations
   # alpha expression

6. Fundamental Data given in the HELP section is not available. Because of that, I am not able to create new alpha. What can I do?

   Answer: Sorry for your inconvenience. We will fix the bugs for fundamental data as soon as possible.

   You can use price and volume to create new alphas. Some good alphas can be generated by this data.

   Thanks for your patience.

7. Whenever I try to use sp.linalg methods, it just produces an error, "Error: No PnL result produced"; the debugger doesn't tell me the details, I've tested this code on my local computer and it seems to work fine. If I comment out the lines that say import scipy.linalg as LA (user defined import statement) and evals, evecs

= LA.eig(matrix(c)), the code works fine. Can you check if sp.linalg methods work fine or not?

Answer: Please find my answer below:

a. As of now, WebSim™ doesn't allow importing modules. You can, however, use numPy and SciPy libraries as they are automatically imported by WebSim™.

So you need to remove this statement from your code:

import scipy.linalg as LA

Also you need to change the call to eig() function to this:

evals, evecs = sp.linalg.eig(matrix(c))

b. eig() function is available to use in WebSim™, but the function requires the input matrix be free from NANs and INFs. The data available in WebSim™ may contain NANs due to data for some company not being available on some day, for example if the company gets de-listed. You need to check for these NANs, and replace them with something more appropriate or remove the stocks containing NANs altogether. For example, if you want to replace all NANs with zeros you may use:

$$c[:] = where(c \mathrel{!=} c, 0, c)$$

c. While the above two would technically make your code error free, it may take a long time to simulate (and eventually time out). The eig() function itself is a time-consuming operation if you consider the fact that it is trying to calculate eigenvalues of a matrix of size around $7,000 \times 7,000$ elements (number of stocks goes up to around 7,000). We are working towards making the Python simulations faster. Meanwhile, you can try to modify your code to calculate eigenvalues of a smaller matrix or perhaps calling the eig() function less frequently.

We understand that figuring these errors requires that the relevant error messages be displayed to the user if a simulation fails. Our team is still working on creating a fix for this bug and it should be ready shortly.

8. I can find only a few mathematic functions and cumulate APIs here. Are there any more resources that can help us know much more about the WebSim™ system and the RF tactics.

Answer: All the functions and data available for use on WebSim™ are given in our FAQ section. Please refer to our Examples under the Help section to learn how to use them. We are working on releasing more functions, datasets, and asset classes soon. We will also be releasing the official WebSim™ documentation that will cover alpha research, more examples, and illustrations. We will keep you updated on the same.

Until then, please feel free to send us a ticket if you have suggestions on how to improve WebSim™ (e.g. for a particular function/new features/ etc. to be added) or technical issues faced while using WebSim™.

9. I'm trying to construct my alpha in Python. I want to be able to refer to day n-1's alpha vector when constructing day n's alpha vector. Is there an easy way to do this?

Answer: In order to store alpha history you need to make a global vector, outside of the "Generate" function. I have attached a sample code. It calculates the following alpha:

$$\text{today's\_alpha} = [(1/\text{close}) + (\text{yesterday's\_alpha})] / 2.$$

Please find the sample code below:

```
closePrice = dr.Getdata("close")
hist = []        #Vector to store alpha history
start = True    #Boolean to determine starting date
def Generate(di,alpha):
# Global variables need to be declared if they're modified within a
   function
global start
global hist
# These 3 lines are to initialize the "hist" vector
if start:
hist = zeros(alpha.shape[0])
start = False
# Computing today's values
wdi = (di-delay)%closePrice.shape[0]
alpha[:] = 1./closePrice[wdi, :]
# Taking average of today's value & yesterday's value, to compute
   final alpha
alpha[:] = 0.5 * (alpha[:] + hist[:])
# Saving today's final alpha value in history vector
hist[:] = alpha[:]
```

OPERATIONS

1. What's the difference between the three market neutralization methods? How do you decide which one is better?

Answer: Market neutralizations determine which groups are used for neutralization of alpha values – all tickers that belong to the same sub-industry, or industry, or simply use the entire universe as one group for this purpose. As for the second question, the correct choice depends on the logic/formula used by the alpha, so there is no specific answer. The results should indicate what to go with.

2. How can you add custom alpha operations and run it along with your alpha expression?

Answer: It is not supported when the code setting is set to expression, but you can realize it using Python.

3. When alpha expression "1" is entered, it returns nothing for every universe. How does one get rid of the NaNs?

Answer: If you look in the Settings dropdown (hover over the gear-shaped icon on the right of the top navigation bar to see this), you'll note that the default neutralization settings is "subindustry." This is why you are seeing NaNs when you use "1" as your expression – the neutralization operation ensures that no position is in fact taken at any point. If you change this setting to "none," you will see the expected results.

4. According to CAPM, $R[i] = B(R[m]) + alpha$ is this the same alpha that we are trying to calculate here? Is it related to Long-Short Market Neutral Strategies that we ignore the beta and just concentrate on alpha or something else?

Answer: WorldQuant's definition of alpha is quite different from what you may have studied (the one related to CAPM).

In WebSim™, an "alpha" refers to a mathematical model or strategy, written as an expression or Python code, which places different bets (weights) on different instruments (stocks), and is expected to be profitable in the long run.

In simple terms, it creates a vector of weights, with each weight corresponding to one of the stocks in the selected universe. These weights may or may not be market neutralized, as per your neutralization setting (market, industry, sub-industry, or none). This creates a portfolio for each day in the simulation period, which can then be used to calculate that day's PnL.

"Alpha" is just a symbolic name and should not be confused with the common definition of alpha, which says that it is a measure of excess or abnormal returns over and above the returns predicted by a strategy (like CAPM).

5. I was testing WebSim™ with the alpha=close*sharesout, with the default settings of universe, etc. To my surprise it gave me POOR result and a negative Sharpe ratio. This is not how Russell 3000 behaved for the past five years, if you could please look into the anomaly.

Answer: Neutralization of default setting is market. In this case, all stocks' weights are made to long or short by market neutralization. So please modify the setting to "None." Please note that the resultant Sharpe and performance will not be good because of the significant dips in the PnL.

ALPHA PERFORMANCE

1. How can I pick up a good expression? What's the threshold for each ratio, such as turnover ratio, max drawdown?

Answer: The criterion for entering an alpha into OS testing is that the Sharpe ratio should exceed a certain threshold. The thresholds are 2.5 and 3.95 for delay 1 and delay 0 alphas, respectively. There are also qualitative words used to describe the performance like "Excellent," "Good," "Inferior," etc. displayed along with the PnL chart (above it), and these are also determined by the Sharpe ratio. (Refer to the FAQ page from the Help menu.)

2. The simulation score is ranked by six levels, Spectacular, Excellent, Good, Average, Inferior, and Poor. What are the criteria that an alpha must satisfy?

Answer: There is an internal threshold which is configurable in terms of Sharpe.

However, the levels given above are another measurement independent of this.

3. Can a user check correlation among his own alphas?

Answer: The correlation is calculated only for alphas which pass the out-sample criterion. It can take several days for the results to show up on My Alphas page.

The results are shown as number of alphas in a particular correlation bracket on the OS tab.

4. When a user submits a new trial, will the result PnL be stored somewhere? Correlation is only available after it passes production, which

is not really convenient. When we improve an idea, we want to check its correlation with the original idea ASAP.

Answer: Currently the daily PnL is NOT stored. Only a summary of the results in the form of the usual statistics is saved. More features that aid alpha development, like the one suggested in the question, will be added.

5. Where's the alpha output vector generated?

Answer: WebSim™ does not show the contents of the alpha vector in the simulation result page.

6. How is the alpha submitted for out-of-sample testing?

Answer: Currently, an alpha is automatically submitted for out-sample testing if it passes the Sharpe threshold as defined earlier in this document.

7. For alphas that get selected for out-sample testing, how soon can I see statistics?

Answer: You can see the statistics in about a week's time because it is done over the weekend.

8. How does the universe affect IR of an alpha?

Answer: Information ratio (IR) of bigger universes should be better than smaller ones. But this is not always true. Some alphas perform better for large stocks, for reasons such as:

a. Data of large stocks is cleaner, i.e. Data has fewer jumps.

b. Behaviors of big stocks are different from small ones.

Alphas in bigger universes are usually easier to develop than smaller universes. However, it is recommended that you develop alphas that can work well on small universes. Small universes have better liquidity.

9. What are the characteristics of a good alpha? How can I maximize my result?

Answer: Originality of idea is essential. The alpha should be robust. An alpha should have a minimum Sharpe of 3.95 for delay 0 alphas, and around 2.5 for delay 1 alphas to be eligible for out-of-sample testing. Also make sure the Returns are high and Turnover is less than 40%, and Drawdown should be kept to a minimum. It's not just about PnL, but also about the impact. Robust performance in liquid universes is needed. OS Sharpe, as well as the drop in performance of IS vs. OS Sharpe, are important.

Alphas with good performance are valuable to us. If you see an alpha in the Out-Sample tab, you can be sure it is valuable.

Think of ideas in arbitrage view. Try different operations (decay, neutralization, etc.). Try new formulas instead of changing one formula. Don't try putting together nonsensical expressions, e.g. adv20 + close, which is essentially volume + price, which doesn't make sense. This can be checked internally by WebSim™ by turning on the Unit Check setting.

Do not overfit parameters. Doing this hurts performance.

Note: Overfitting here refers to changing the alpha expression slightly in a nonsensical way, just to get a good IS Sharpe; e.g. slightly changing the constants in the expression, changing the power of a parameter from 2 to 2.5, static flip sign of some sectors, etc. This shouldn't be done since it will inevitably fail the OS test constraints.

Note: For all queries/suggestions/feedbacks, please send an email via WebSim's™ contact page. For any technical issues, users must report it along with the browser they were using and its version, as well as the precise time at which they last encountered the issue to the WebSim™ team so that they can pinpoint the relevant log messages.

33
Suggested Readings
By the WebSim™ Team

This chapter includes reference sections with a list of academic/professional papers that can be used as a source of alpha ideas.

Note that the third-party links mentioned below are for reference purpose and user's convenience only. These third-party sites may have their own terms of use and the reader is strongly urged to read and abide by them.

FINANCE BASICS

There is also a lot of information available on the web on the terms included in this section. We will provide links to additional information where possible but the reader is strongly encouraged to do a web search or research these terms on public open sources such as Wikipedia, Google Scholar, Investopedia, etc.

1. Active Portfolio Management
   Source: Active Portfolio Management: A Quantitative Approach for Producing Superior Returns and Controlling Risks, by Richard Grinold and Ronald Kahn
   Comment: Foundations, expected returns and valuations, and implementations.
2. Market Neutral
   Comment: Defines the terms market neutral, equity market neutral, and provides illustrations.

3. Capital Asset Pricing Model
   Source: http://papers.ssrn.com/sol3/papers.cfm?abstract_id=440920
   Comment: Gives an introduction to CAPM, its formula, security market
       line, asset pricing, asset-specific required return, risk and diversifica-
       tion, efficient frontier, market portfolio, assumptions of CAPM.
4. Fama and French Model
   Source: http://www.moneychimp.com/articles/risk/multifactor.htm
   Source: http://www.portfoliosolutions.com/our-process-2/
       confidencemap-planning/understanding-risk/
   Comment: This gives an introduction, portfolio analysis, investing
       for the future, and conclusions inferred from analyzing the Fama-
       French model.
5. Market Efficiency
   Source: http://www.investopedia.com/articles/02/101502.asp
   Comment: Explains what market efficiency is; the effect, challenge,
       and degrees of efficiency, and the bottom line.
6. Information Ratio
   Source: http://www.cfapubs.org/doi/abs/10.2469/ipmn.v2011.n1.7
   Source: http://seekingalpha.com/article/63911-clarifying-the-
       information-ratio-and-sharpe-ratio
   Comment: Formula and definition of IR, comparing Sharpe and
       information ratio.
7. Corporate Fundamental Analysis
   Source: https://www.tradeking.com/education/stocks/fundamental-
       analysis-explained
   Source: http://www.euroinvestor.com/ei-news/2012/02/12/stock-
       school-5-important-elements-in-fundamental-analysis/15694
   Comment: Gives introduction, procedure, its strength and weaknesses,
       and five important elements in fundamental analysis.

CLASSICAL PAPERS FOR QUANT RESEARCH

1. The Cross-Section of Expected Stock Returns
   Source: http://www.bengrahaminvesting.ca/Research/Papers/French/
       The_Cross-Section_of_Expected_Stock_Returns.pdf
   Comment: This is the famous "Fama-French" paper, which proposed
       the "Fama-French" factor, and the basics of cross-sectional equity
       research methods.

2. Size, Value, and Momentum in International Stock Returns
   Source: http://papers.ssrn.com/sol3/papers.cfm?abstract_id=1720139
   Comment: The "Fama-French" factors applied in international markets.
3. Value and Momentum Everywhere
   Source: http://schwert.ssb.rochester.edu/f532/AMP12.pdf
   Comment: A good introduction to value and momentum; they can generate abnormal returns for individual stocks within several countries, across country equity indices, government bonds, currencies, and commodities.
4. Mean Reversion in Stock Prices: Evidence and Implications
   Source: http://papers.ssrn.com/sol3/papers.cfm?abstract_id=227278
   Comment: One of the earliest papers reflecting the mean-reversion nature of stock prices.
5. Price Momentum and Trading Volume
   Source: http://technicalanalysis.org.uk/volume/LeSw00.pdf
   Comment: Gives insight to what the role of volume is: past trading volume provides an important link between "momentum" and "value" strategies.

OVERFITTING RISK AND WHERE TO FIND ALPHAS

1. Anomalies and Market Efficiency
   Source: http://citeseerx.ist.psu.edu/viewdoc/download?doi=10.1.1.1
   97.5770&rep=rep1&type=pdf
2. Seven Market Anomalies Investors Should Know
   Source: http://www.investopedia.com/articles/financial-theory/11/
   trading-with-market-anomalies.asp
3. What You See May Not Be What You Get: A Brief, Nontechnical Introduction to Overfitting in Regression-Type Models
   Source: http://people.duke.edu/~mababyak/papers/babyakregression
   .pdf
4. The Probability of Backtest Overfitting
   Source: http://papers.ssrn.com/sol3/papers.cfm?abstract_id=2326253
5. What Happened to the Quants in August 2007? Evidence from Factors and Transactions Data
   Source: http://www.argentumlux.org/documents/august07b_2.pdf

ALPHA RESEARCH PAPERS

Allen, E., Larson, C. and R.G. Sloan (2011). Accrual reversals, earnings and stock returns. Working paper, University of California, Berkeley.

Ang, A., Hodrick, R.J., Xing, Y. and Zhang, X. (2006). The cross-section of volatility and expected returns. *Journal of Finance* LXI, 1. p. 259–299.

Bali, T.G. and N. Cakici (2008). Idiosyncratic volatility and the cross section of expected returns. *Journal of Financial & Quantitative Analysis* 43, 1. p. 29–58.

Bali, T.G. and A. Hovakimian (2009). Volatility spreads and expected stock returns. *Management Science* 55, 11. p. 1797–1812.

Bandyopadhyay, S.P., Huang, A.G. and T.S. Wirjanto (2010). The accrual volatility anomaly. Working paper, University of Waterloo.

Basu, S. (1975). The information content of price-earnings ratios. *Financial Management* 4, 2. p. 53–64.

Bauman, W.S. and R. Dowen (1988). Growth projections and common stock returns. *Financial Analysts Journal*, July/August.

Beneish, M.D. and D.C. Nichols (2009). Identifying overvalued equity. Working paper, Indiana University.

Boehme, R.D., Danielsen, B.R., Kumar, P., and S.M.Sorescu (2009). Idiosyncratic risk and the cross-section of stock returns: Merton (1987) meets Miller (1977). *Journal of Financial Markets* 12. p. 438–468.

Bourguignon, F. and M. de Jong (2006). The importance of being value. *Journal of Portfolio Management* Spring. p. 74–79.

Daniel, K. and S. Titman (1997). Evidence on the characteristics of cross sectional variation in stock returns. *Journal of Finance* 52. p. 1–33.

Fama, E.F. and J.D. MacBeth (1973). Risk, retrun and equilibrium: Empirical tests. *Journal of Political Economy* 81. p. 607–636.

Kaplan, S.N. and L. Zingales (1997). Do investment-cash flow sensitivities provide useful measures of financing constrains? *Quarterly Journal of Economics* 112. p. 169–215.

Livdan, D., Sapriza H. and L. Zhang (2009). Financially constrained stock returns. *Journal of Finance* 64. p. 1827–1862.

Parker, J.A. and C. Julliard (2005). Consumption risk and the cross section of expected returns. *Journal of Political Economy* 113. p. 186–222.

Spiess, D.K. and J. Affleck-Graves (1999). The long-run performance of stock returns following debt offerings. *Journal of Financial Economics* 54. p. 45–73.

Note: Please refer to our website at worldquantchallenge.com for the monthly updated reading list.

PART V
A Final Word

34
The Seven Habits of Highly Successful Quants

By Richard Hu

A quant is also referred to as the "Rocket Scientist on Wall Street," and that phrase conjures up an image of someone who is smart, well-educated, and very highly paid – perhaps millions of dollars a year. In typical buy-side quantitative investment firms, the work environment is collegial and professional; and it is a place where you will have plenty of opportunities to gain new knowledge. Therefore, it's not hard to understand why many top engineering and science graduates from the best universities in the world want to become quants.

Over the last 10 years, I have managed hundreds of quants, and I have also talked to thousands of aspiring quants during many recruiting events in over 10 countries. A frequent question that comes up is: What does it take to become a successful quant?

In order to answer this question, we surveyed and interviewed many top-tier quants. We identified the following seven habits as the most important reasons for their success.

1. Willing to put in the extra effort

   Highly successful quants are willing to put in the necessary extra efforts to reach their success. If failure is the mother of success, then extra effort is the father.

   I had once hired an extremely smart young man from a top-tier university. In the interviews, he was able to solve our very difficult analytical questions at such a fast speed that we suspected he had seen those questions before. Since he did so well in all our interviews, we decided to take some time to make up a set of brand new, very tough questions for him; yet again he aced them at lightning speed. We were so pleased that we found such a gem. After he came on board, however, I discovered he had a serious flaw. He did not work hard. He would party in the evenings and stay out late at nights, such that he would often wake up late and run into the office at 10 a.m., while others would have already started at 8 a.m. When I talked to him about this, he would shape up for a while. Then he would be back to his old ways and fall behind like a sleeping hare. He never became the best.

On the other hand, I have hired people who are smart but not necessarily the smartest. I have seen them among the first ones to come to the office and among the last ones to leave – day after day, month after month, and year after year. Over time, such people slowly yet steadily got ahead of the others, one at a time, and they eventually became among our top performers. Of course, among the people I've seen, those who are both the smartest and hardest working are bound to become successful quickly. But given a choice between steady extra effort and higher raw IQ, steady extra effort wins.

2. Always make sensible changes, don't just try to fit the model to the data

Alpha research is an experimental process during which one comes up with many hypotheses and tries many experiments. Many of the hypotheses and experiments will not result in excellent results. When the results are not good enough, the easy thing to do is to tune the model parameters until it passes a certain minimum threshold. This type of alpha does not perform well in the real market. Successful quants will try to figure out the reasons for the suboptimal results, and try to make refinements that make sense. Such alphas will be more likely to perform well in the real market.

3. Eager to experiment with new ideas

Successful quants are interested in exploring new ideas and new data. Sometimes, in order to explore new territories, more preparatory or foundation work will need to be done; the successful quants are willing to do that work. If one waits until all the roadblocks have been removed, then much of the treasure will have already been found by others.

4. Do value-added work

When creating alphas, it is easier to create an alpha that is a slight variation of other proven alphas, and it is harder to come up with an alpha based on a new idea. However, it is the latter that adds more value to portfolio management. Successful quants put in more effort in coming up with alphas based on new ideas.

5. Have a strong sense of urgency

The most successful quants have a strong urgency to get things done. When they have an idea, they can't wait to try it. They are always thinking about alpha research, are very quick to follow through, and are very active mentally.

6. Form synergistic teams

Many highly successful quants try to form teams with other good quants, whom they like and trust. Teammates discuss alpha ideas, share research tools, help each other through temporary setbacks, and break the monotony of solitary research. Through this teaming process, they become more productive, end up with more results, and create a more enjoyable working environment for themselves.

7. Set high targets

For the final habit, I'll use an old saying: "Shoot for the moon. Even if you miss, you'll land among the stars."

These are the seven habits of a highly successful quant. Follow them well, and one day you may find that a princely life of a highly successful quant suits you to a tee.

References

JOURNAL ARTICLES (PRINTED)

Amihud, Y. and Mendelson, H. (1986) Asset Pricing and the Bid-Ask Spread. *Journal of Financial Economics*. 17. p. 223–249.

Abarbanell, J. and Bushee, B. (1997) Financial Statement Analysis, Future Earnings and Stock Prices. *Journal of Accounting Research*. 35. p. 1–24.

Black, F. (1975) Fact and Fantasy in the Use of Options. *Financial Analysts Journal*. 31. p. 36–72.

Bollen, N.P. and Whaley, R.E. (2004) Does Net Buying Pressure Affect the Shape of Implied Volatility Functions? *The Journal of Finance*. 59. p. 711–753.

Bertsimas, D., Lauprete, G.J. and Samarov, A. (2004) Shortfall as a Risk Measure: Properties, Optimization and Applications. *Journal of Economic Dynamics and Control*. 28, Issue 7. p. 1353–1381.

Butterworth, S. (1930) On the Theory of Filter Amplifiers. *Wireless Engineer* (also called *Experimental Wireless and Wireless Engineer*). 7. p. 17–20.

Chan, L., Jegadeesh, N. and Sougiannis, T. (1996) Momentum Strategies. *The Journal of Finance*. 51. p. 1681–1713.

Chan, L., Lakonishok, J. and Sougiannis, T. (2001) The Stock Market Valuation of Research and Development Expenditures. *Journal of Finance*. 6. p. 1681.

Cremers, M. and Weinbaum, D. (Forthcoming) Deviations from Put-Call Parity and Stock Return Predictability. *Journal of Financial and Quantitative Analysis*. Forthcoming.

Fama, E. and French, K. (1992) The Cross-Section of Expected Stock Returns. *The Journal of Finance*. 47(2). p. 427–466.

Francis, J., Schipper, K. and Vincent, L. (2002) Earnings Announcements and Competing Information. *Journal of Accounting and Economics*. 33(3). p. 313–342.

Frankel, R., Kothari. S.P. and Weber, J. (2006) Determinants of the Informativeness of Analyst Research. *Journal of Accounting and Economics*. 41(1). p. 29–54.

Freund, Y. and Schapire, R.E. (1999) A Short Introduction to Boosting. *Journal of Japanese Society for Artificial Intelligence*. 14(5). p. 771–781.

Jegadeesh, N. and Titman, S. (1993) Returns to Buying Winners and Selling Losers: Implications for Stock Market Efficiency. *The Journal of Finance*. 48(1). p. 65–91.

Lintner, J. (1965) The Valuation of Risk Assets and the Selection of Risky Investments in Stock Portfolios and Capital Budgets. *Review of Economics and Statistics*. 47 (1). p. 13–37.

Lin, H. and McNichols, M. F. (1998) Underwriting Relationships, Analysts' Earnings Forecasts and Investment Recommendations. *Journal of Accounting and Economics*. 25. p. 101–127.

Markowitz, H. (1952) Portfolio Selection. *The Journal of Finance*. 7(1). p. 77–91.

Mossin, J. (1966) Equilibrium in a Capital Asset Market. *Econometrica*. 34(4). p. 768–783.

Michaely, R. and Womack, K.L. (1999) Conflict of Interest and the Credibility of Underwriter Anaylyst Recommendations. *Review of Financial Studies*. 12. p. 653–686.

Nissim, D. and Penman, S. (2003) Financial Statement Analysis of Leverage and How It Informs About Profitability and Price-to-Book Ratios. *Review of Accounting Studies*. 8. p. 531–560.

Ofek, E., Richardson, M. and Whitelaw, R.F. (2004) Limited Arbitrage and Short Sales Restrictions: Evidence from the Option Market. *Journal of Financial Economics*. 74. p. 305–342.

Pastor, L. and Stambaugh, R. (2003) Liquidity Risk ad Expected Stock Returns. *Journal of Political Economy*. 111(3). p. 642–685.

Piotroski, J. (2000) The Use of Historical Financial Information to Separate Winners from Losers. *The Journal of Accounting Research*. 28. p. 141.

Sharpe, W. (1964) Capital Asset Prices: A Theory of Market Equilibrium under Conditions of Risk. *The Journal of Finance*. 19(3). p. 425–442.

Xing, Y., Zhang, X. and Zhao, R. (2010) What Does Individual Option Volatility Smirk Tell Us about Future Equity Returns? *Journal of Financial and Quantitative Analysis*. 45. p. 335–367.

JOURNAL ARTICLES (ELECTRONIC/ONLINE)

Bailey, D.H., Borwein, J.M., Lopez de Prado, M. and Zhu, Q.J. (2014a) The Probability of Backtest Overfitting. [Online] Social Science Research Network 2326253. Available from SSRN: http://ssrn.com/abstract=2326253 [Accessed: December 3, 2014].

Bailey, D.H., Borwein, J.M., Lopez de Prado, M. and Zhu, Q.J. (2014b) Pseudo-Mathematics and Financial Charlatanism: The Effects of Backtest Overfitting on Out-of-Sample Performance. *Notices of the American Mathematical Society*. 61(5), May 2014. p. 458–471. [Online] Social Science Research Network. Abstract 2308569. Available from: http://ssrn.com/abstract=2308569 [Accessed: December 3, 2104].

Beaudan, P. (2013) Telling the Good from the Bad and the Ugly: How to Evaluate Backtested Investment Strategies. [Online] Social Science Research Network. Abstract 2346600. Available from: http://ssrn.com/abstract=2346600 [Accessed: December 3, 2014].

Burns, P. (2006) Random Portfolios for Evaluating Trading Strategies. [Online] Social Science Research Network. Abstract 881735. Available from: http://ssrn.com/abstract=881735 [Accessed: December 3, 2014].

Fodor, A., Krieger, K. and Doran J.S. (2010) Do Option Open-Interest Changes Foreshadow Future Equity Returns? [Online] Social Science Research Network, Abstract 1634065. Available from: http://ssrn.com/abstract=1634065 [Accessed December 8, 2014].

Garleanu, N., Pedersen, L.H. and Poteshman, A.M. (2009) Demand-Based Option Pricing. EFA 2005 Moscow Meeting Paper. [Online] SSRN, Abstract 676501. Available from: http://ssrn.com/abstract=676501 [Accessed: December 8, 2014].

Harvey, C.R., Liu, Y. and Zhu, H. (2014) ...and the Cross-Section of Expected Returns. [Online] Social Science Research Network. Abstract 2249314. Available from: http://ssrn.com/abstract=2249314 [Accessed: December 3, 2014].

Harrington, A. (Date Unknown) Hands-On Python: A Tutorial Introduction for Beginners Python 3.1 Version. [Online] Neurogenetics at UT Health Science Center. Available from: http://www.nervenet.org/pdf/python3handson.pdf [Accessed: December 9, 2014].

Hirshleifer, D. and Shumway, T. (June 2003) Good Day Sunshine: Stock Returns and the Weather. *The Journal of Finance.* 58(3). p. 1009–1031. [Online] JSTOR. 3094570. Available from: http://www.jstor.org/stable/3095570 [Accessed: December 4, 2014].

Jin, W., Livnat, J. and Zhang, Y. (2012) Option Prices Leading Equity Prices: Do Option Traders Have an Information Advantage. *Journal of Accounting Research*, Forthcoming. [Online] SSRN. Abstract 1982227. Available from: http://ssrn.com/abstract=1982227 [Accessed: December 8, 2014].

Johnson, T.L. and So, E.C. (2011) The Option to Stock Volume Ration and Future Returns. [Online] Social Science Research Network. Abstract 1624062. Available from: http://ssrn.comabstract=1624062 [Accessed: December 8, 2014].

Kamstra, M.J., Kramer, L.A. and Levi, M.D. (October 2002) Winter Blues: A SAD Stock Market Cycle. *Federal Reserve Bank of Atlanta Working Paper No. 2002-13a; Saunder School of Business Working Paper.* [Online] SSRN Database Abstract 208622. Available from: http://ssrn.com/abstract=208622.

Khandani, A. and Lo, A. (2007) What Happened to the Quants in August 2007. [Online] MIT Papers. August 7. Available from: http://web.mit.edu/alo/www/Papers/august07.pdf [Accessed: December 4, 2014].

Lopez de Prado, M. (2013) What to Look for in a Backtest [Online]. Social Science Research Network. Abstract 2308682. Available from SSRN: http://ssrn.com/abstract=2308682 [Accessed: December 3, 2014].

Matloff, N. (2011) Fast Lane to Python. [Online] University of California, Davis. Available from: http://heather.cs.ucdavis.edu/~matloff/Python/PLN/FastLanePython.pdf [Accessed: December 9, 2014].

Mohanram, P.S. (2004) Separating Winners from Losers Among Low Book-to-Market Stocks using Financial Statement Analysis. [Online] SSRN. Abstract 403180. Available from: http://ssrn.com/abastract=403180 [Accessed: December 8, 2014].

Mohr, M. (2005) A Trend-Cycle (-Season). *European Central Bank.* [Online] Working Paper Series. No. 499/July 2005. Available from: https://www.ecb.europa.eu/pub/pdf/scpwps/ecbwp499.pdf [Accessed December 4, 2014].

Preis, T., Moat, H.S. and Stanley, H.E. (April 2013) Quantifying Trading Behavior in Financial Markets Using *Google* Trends. *Scientific Reports* 3. [Online] Article Number 1684. Available from: http://www.nature.com/srep/2013/130425/srep01684/full/srep01684.html.

Roll, R., Schwartz, E. and Subrahmanyam, A. (2009) O/S: The Relative Trading Activity in Options and Stock. *Journal of Financial Economics.* [Online] SSRN Abstract=1410091. Available from: http://ssrn.com/abstract=1410091 [Accessed December 15, 2014].

Schorfheide, F. and Wolpin, K.I. (2012) On the Use of Holdout Samples for Model Selection. *American Economic Review – Papers and Proceedings.* 102(3). p. 477–481. Available from: http://sites.sas.upenn.edu/schorf/publications [Accessed: December 3, 2014].

Sloan, R.G., Khimich, N.V. and Dechow, P.M. (2011) The Accural Anomaly. [Online] Social Science Research Network. Abstract 1793364. Available from SSRN: http://ssrn.com/abstract=1793364 [Accessed: June 2, 2015].

Spearman, C. (1987) The Proof and Measurement of Association between Two Things. By C. Spearman 1904. *The American Journal of Psychology.* 100(3–4). p. 441–471.

BOOKS

Downey, A.B. (2012) *Think Python.* O'Reilly. [Online] Available from: http://www.greenteapress.com/thinkpython [Accessed December 10, 2014].

Graham, B. and Dodd, D. (1940) *Security Analysis.* McGraw-Hill Book Company.

Huber, P.J. (2003) *Robust Statistics.* Wiley Series in Probability and Statistics.

Hull, J. (2008) *Options, Futures and Other Derivatives*. Pearson Prentice Hall.

Kahneman, D. (2011) *Thinking, Fast and Slow*. Farrar, Straus and Giroux.

Lefevre, E. (1923) *Reminiscences of a Stock Operator*. John Wiley & Sons.

Popper, K. (1959) *The Logic of Scientific Discovery*. Translation of *Logik der Forschung*. London: Hutchinson.

Mertz, D. (2006) *Text Processing in Python*. Addison Wesley. [Online] Gnosis Software. Available from: http://gnosis.cx/TPiP.

Rousseeuw, P.J. and Leroy, A.M. (1987, republished in paperback in 2003) *Robust Regression and Outlier Detection*. Wiley.

Swaroop, C.H. (2014) *A Byte of Python*. [Online] Available from: http://www.swaroopch.com/notes/python.

UNPUBLISHED MANUSCRIPTS/WORKING PAPER SERIES

Beneish, M.D. and Nichols, D.C. (2009) Identifying Overvalued Equity. Johnson School Research Paper Series No. 09-09. [Online] SSRN. Abstract 1134818. Available from: http://ssrn.com/abstract=1134818 [Accessed: December 8, 2014].

Bradshaw, M.T., Hutton, A.P., Marcus, A.J. and Tehranian, H. (2010) Opacity, Crash Risk, and the Option Smirk Curve. Working Paper. Boston College. [Online] SSRN Abstract 1640733. Available from: http://ssrn.com/abstract=1640733 [Accessed: December 8, 2014].

Treynor, J. (1962) Toward a Theory of Market Value of Risky Assets. Unpublished manuscript.

Van Buskirk, A. (2011) Volatility Skew, Earnings Announcements and the Predictability of Crashes. Working Paper Series. [Online] SSRN. Abstract 1740513. Available from: http://ssrn.com/abstract=1740513 [Accessed: December 8, 2014].

WEBSITES

Bloomberg (1981) [Online] Available from: http://www.bloomberg.com [Accessed: December 12, 2014].

CFA Institute (2014) *Publications: Financial Analysts Journal*. [Online] Available from: http://www.cfapubs.org/loi/faj [Accessed: December 11, 2014].

Codeacademy (2014) *Python*. [Online] Available from: http://www.codeacademy.com/tracks/python [Accessed: December 9, 2014].

Cornell University Library (2014) *ArXiv* [Online] Available from: http://arvix.org [Accessed: 12th December 2014].

Elsevier (2014) *Journal of Banking and Finance*. [Online] Available from: http://www.journals.elsevier.com/journal-of-banking-and-finance [Accessed: December 11, 2014].

Elsevier (2014) *Journal of Corporate Finance*. [Online] Available from: http://www.journals.elsevier.com/journal-of-corporate-finance [Accessed: December 11, 2014].

Elsevier (2014) *Journal of Empirical Finance*. [Online] Available from: http://www.journals.elsevier.com/journal-of-empirical-finance [Accessed: December 11, 2014].

Elsevier (2014) *Journal of Financial Intermediation*. [Online] Available from: http://www.journals.elsevier.com/journal-of-financial-intermediation [Accessed: December 11, 2014].

Elsevier (2014) *Journal of Financial Markets*. [Online] Available from: http://www.journals.elsevier.com/journal-of-financial-markets [Accessed: December 11, 2014].

Elsevier (2014) *Journal of International Money and Finance*. [Online] Available from: http://www.journals.elsevier.com/journal-of-international-money-and-finance [Accessed: December 11, 2014].

Elsevier (2014) *Pacific-Basin Finance Journal*. [Online] Available from: http://www.journals.elsevier.com/pacific-basin-finance-journal [Accessed: December 11, 2014].

Google (2014) *Google Finance*. [Online] http://www.google.com/finance [Accessed: December 12, 2014].

Google (2014) *Google Scholar*. [Online] Available from: http://scholar.google.com [Accessed: December 11, 2014].

Incredible Charts (2001–2004) *Indicator Basics: How to Use Technical Indicators.* [Online] Available from: http://www.incrediblecharts.com/indicators/indicators.php [Accessed: December 9, 2014].

Institutional Investor Journals (2014) *Journal of Portfolio Management.* [Online] Available from: http://www.iijournals.com/toc/jpm/current [Accessed: December 11, 2014].

Investopedia (2014) *Identifying Market Trends.* [Online] Available from: http://investopedia.com/articles/technical/03/060303.asp [Accessed: December 9, 2014].

Jstor (2000–2014) *The Journal of Business.* [Online] Available from: http://www.jstor.org/page/journal/jbusiness/about.html [Accessed: December 11, 2014].

Lagadec, P. (2009) *Decalage: A Mini Python Tutorial.* [Online] Available from: http://www.decalage.info/files/mini_python_tutorial_0.03.pdf   [Accessed: December 10, 2014].

Morningstar (2014) [Online] Available from: http://www.moringstar.com.

NasdaqTrader (2014) *Options Market Share Statistics.* [Online] Available from: http://www.nasdaqtrader.com/trader.aspx?id=marketsharenom [Accessed December 4, 2014].

NumPy (2008–2009) *Reference.* [Online] SciPy Community. Available from: http://docs.scipy.org/doc/numpy/reference [Accessed: December 10, 2014].

Numpy (2013) *Numpy Developers.* [Online] Available from: http://www.numpy.org [Accessed: December 9, 2014].

Pilgrim, M. (2000, 2001) *Dive into Python.* [Online] Available from: http://www.diveintopython.net [Accessed: December 8, 2014].

Pointal, L. (2005–2006) *Python 2.4 Quick Reference Card.* [Online] Available from: http://www2-pcmdi.llnl.gov/cdat/manuals/Python%202.4%20Quick%20Reference%20Card.pdf [Accessed: December 9, 2014].

Renater. The Higher Education and Research Forge (Date Unknown) *SourceSup Documentation.* [Online] Available from: https://sourcesup.renater.fr/projects/scientific-py [Accessed: December 10, 2014].

SciPy (2008–2009) *NumPy User Guide.* [Online] The SciPy Community. Available from: http://docs.scipy.org/doc/numpy/user [Accessed: December 10, 2014].

SciPy (2008–2009) *Statistical Functions (SciPy Stats)*. [Online] SciPy Community 2014. Available from: http://docs.scipy.org/doc/scipy/reference/stats.html.

SciPy (2014) [Online] Available from: http://www.scipy.org [Accessed: December 10, 2014].

SEC (2000) *Final Rule: Selective Disclosure and Inside Trading*. [Online] Available from: http://www.sec.gov/rules/final/33-7881.htm [Accessed December 17, 2014].

Seeking Alpha (2014) [Online] Available from: http://seekingalpha.com/ [Accessed: December 10, 2014].

Sloan R.G., Khimich N.V., Dechow, P.M. (2011) *The Accural Anomaly* [Online]. Social Science Research Network. Abstract 1793364. Available from SSRN: http://ssrn.com/abstract=1793364 [Accessed: June 2, 2015].

Social Science Research Network (2014) [Online] Available from: http://www.ssrn.cm/en/ [Accessed: December 10, 2014].

Springer (2014) *Review of Quantitative Finance and Accounting*. [Online] Available from: http://www.springer.com/business+%26+management/finance/journal/11156 [Accessed: December 11, 2014].

Stock Charts (1999–2014) *Technical Indicators and Overlays*. [Online] Available from: http://stockcharts.com/school/doku.php?id=chart_school:technical_indicators [Accessed: December 10, 2014].

The National Bureau of Economic Research (2014) [Online] Available from: http://www.nber.org [Accessed: December 12, 2014].

Time (2014) *The 25 Best Financial Blogs*. [Online] Available from: http://content.time.com/time/specials/packages/completelist/0,29569,2057116,00.html [Accessed: December 17, 2014].

Tutorialspoint (2014) *Python-Quick Guide*. [Online] Available from: http://www.tutorialspoint.com/python/python_quick_guide.htm [Accessed: December 10, 2014].

University of Washington Web Server (2014) *Journal of Financial and Quantitative Analysis*. [Online] Available from: http://depts.washington.edu/jfqa [Accessed: December 11, 2014].

Wall Street Journals (2014) [Online] Available from: www.onlin.wsj.com [Accessed: December 12, 2014].

Wiley Online Library (1999–2014) *Financial Research*. [Online] Available from: http://onlinelibrary.wiley.com/journal/10.1111/(ISSN)1475-6803 [Accessed: December 11, 2014].

Wiley Online Library (1999–2014) *Financial Review*. [Online] Available from: http://onlinelibrary.wiley.com/journal/10.1111/(ISSN)1540-6288 [Accessed: December 11, 2014].

Wiley Online Library (1999–2014) *Journal of Futures Markets*. [Online] Available from: http://onlinelibrary.wiley.com/journal/10.1002/(ISSN)1096-9934 [Accessed: December 11, 2014].

Wilmott (1999–2014) [Online] Available from: http://www.wilmott.com [Accessed: December 10, 2014].

WolframMathWorld (2014) *Reuleaux Triangle*. [Online] Available from: http://mathworld.wolfram.com/images/gifts/reuleaux.gif [Accessed December 4, 2014].

WorldQuantChallenge (2014) [Online] Available from: https://websim .worlfquantchallenge.com [Accessed: December 10, 2014].

Yahoo Finance (2014) *AAPL*. [Online] Available from: http://www.finance .yahoo.com [Accessed: December 11, 2014].

ONLINE BLOGS

Larrabee, D. (2014) A Little Industry Experience May Make You a Better Analyst. [Online] CFA Institute Blog. Available from: http://blogs.cfainstitute.org/investor/2014/02/18/career-matters-prior-industry-experience-improves-odds-of-success-for-wall-street-analysts [Accessed December 12, 2014].

PUBLIC REPORTS

Options Clearing Corporation (2013) *Annual Report 2013*. [Online] Available from: http://www.optionsclearing.com/components/docs/about/annual-reports/occ_2013_annual_report.pdf [Accessed December 4, 2014].

U.S. Commodity Futures (2014) *Commitments of Traders*. [Online] Available from: http://www.cftc.gov/marketreports/commitmentsoftraders/index.htm [Accessed: December 10, 2014].

Index